Something Old, Something New

Army Leader Development in a Dynamic Environment

Henry A. Leonard, J. Michael Polich, Jeffrey D. Peterson, Ronald E. Sortor, S. Craig Moore

Prepared for the United States Army

RAND ARROYO CENTER

The research described in this report was sponsored by the United States Army under Contract No. DASW01-01-C-0003.

Library of Congress Cataloging-in-Publication Data

Something old, something new : Army leader development in a dynamic environment / Henry A. Leonard . . . [et al.].
p. cm.
"MG-281."
Includes bibliographical references.
ISBN 0-8330-3887-7 (pbk.)
1. United States. Army—Officers—Training of. 2. Command of troops. 3. Leadership—United States. I. Leonard, Henry A.

UB413.S65 2006
355.5'50973—dc22

2005034812

The RAND Corporation is a nonprofit research organization providing objective analysis and effective solutions that address the challenges facing the public and private sectors around the world. RAND's publications do not necessarily reflect the opinions of its research clients and sponsors.

Published 2006 by the RAND Corporation
1776 Main Street, P.O. Box 2138, Santa Monica, CA 90407-2138
1200 South Hayes Street, Arlington, VA 22202-5050
201 North Craig Street, Suite 202, Pittsburgh, PA 15213-1516
RAND URL: http://www.rand.org/
To order RAND documents or to obtain additional information, contact
Distribution Services: Telephone: (310) 451-7002;
Fax: (310) 451-6915; Email: order@rand.org

Preface

This report examines the nature of demands on Army officers in the contemporary operating environment and ways in which those demands may affect future leader development.

Compared with the relative stability that characterized the world situation over many preceding decades, the operational picture in recent years has become much more variable—encompassing sharply different operations in unfamiliar locations, such as Somalia, Bosnia, Kosovo, Haiti, and Kuwait. Those operations were followed by the onset of international terrorism directed at the United States, and the ensuing conflicts in Afghanistan and Iraq. These developments spell profound changes in missions and environments, affecting Army leaders in ways that are yet to be determined.

The research project on which this report is based arose from dual concerns about the possible effects of the changes in the operational environment and a closely related development, the Army's ongoing transformation of its structure and posture. As Army planners recognized early on, the emerging environment calls for different operational activities in different contexts, compared with historical norms. Simultaneously, the Army had embarked on planning for new types of units with novel organizational structures and equipment (such as Stryker brigades and eventual conversion to future combat systems).[1] These changes prompted questions about how best to prepare future leaders for the new demands that will inevitably be placed on them.

This report describes RAND Arroyo Center analysis and findings regarding three major topics: the general attributes and intellectual qualities required by leaders in the modern environment; specific operational skills and depth that the new environment demands of leaders; and the extent to which career paths can provide additional time and experience in operational units while still meeting all of the other demands on the officer corps.

---

[1] Since this research was conducted, still other structural changes have been announced, such as the initiative to modularize combat units and create different supporting entities.

This research was sponsored by the Chief of Staff, U.S. Army Training and Doctrine Command, and was conducted in RAND Arroyo Center's Manpower and Training Program. RAND Arroyo Center, part of the RAND Corporation, is a federally funded research and development center sponsored by the United States Army.

For more information on RAND Arroyo Center, contact the Director of Operations (telephone 310-393-0411, extension 6419; FAX 310-451-6952; email Marcy_Agmon@rand.org), or visit Arroyo's web site at http://www.rand.org/ard/.

Contents

Figures

Tables

Summary

Background

Over the past two decades many aspects of military operations have changed profoundly, with the potential for equally profound effects on the things that Army leaders must know and do. The tangible threat of the Soviet Union has been replaced by amorphous, changing, and ill-defined threats and challenges. Simultaneously, the focus has shifted toward stability operations, support operations, and military operations other than war. As a result, considerations that once were peripheral now often take center stage. These changes have created a dynamic situation—volatile, unpredictable, and novel in many respects—making the conduct of military operations more complex and varied than in the past.

The Department of Defense and the Army have taken many steps to adapt to these changes, but so far that adaptation has centered largely on the more tangible elements and mechanics of war: weapons, logistics, doctrine, unit organization, and basing. Less attention was paid at first to how the contemporary environment affects soldiers and especially *leaders*. Since it seems likely that the new environment may call for officers to have different skills, greater knowledge in certain areas, or a different intellectual orientation toward command and decision making, we undertook an examination of how recent changes in the operational environment might have affected leadership requirements. We then assessed the degree to which the Army may need to make corresponding changes in how officers are educated, developed, and prepared for the fluidity of the contemporary environment.[1]

Something Old: Foundations of Military Leadership

Many of the general attributes that the Army seeks in officers reflect timeless values that will remain at the core of leadership. These enduring attributes include character

[1] Parallel concerns may apply to noncommissioned officers and other leaders. However, we limited our scope to commissioned officers.

and values as well as many basic military technical and operational skills (the "something old" in our title). The Army's long-standing formulation of leadership's core (Department of the Army, 1999) is built around three critical aspects:

- What the leader must *Be* (the persona, primarily character);
- What he or she must *Know* (from very general to very specific areas of knowledge and skill, over a range of disciplines); and
- What he or she must *Do* (the kinds of actions leaders must take to make their organizations accomplish their tasks and function effectively).

The Army's doctrine, in common with other treatments of leadership, particularly emphasizes character as essential to success in leadership. That doctrine lists seven values that form the essence of military character, the foundation of what the leader must Be: loyalty, duty, respect, selfless service, honor, integrity, personal courage. The other aspects of what the leader must Be fall into three categories: mental, physical, and emotional. The mental category includes will, self-discipline, initiative, judgment, self-confidence, intelligence, and cultural awareness. The physical dimension includes physical fitness, general good health, and military and professional bearing. The most important emotional attributes are identified as self-control, balance, and stability. No doubt the value of these attributes will endure. Nevertheless, even at this level of generality, some attributes may need to be developed in different ways or to a different degree. For example, cultural awareness is taking on greater importance throughout the Army, and particularly at lower levels in the chain of command. Likewise intellectual acuity, while always a desirable trait, is being applied in different decision-making processes to deal with new challenges. Thus, it is now more important to develop officers with well-grounded intellectual and critical thinking abilities, practiced intensively across a range of situations.

The other two elements of the Army's leadership construct cover what the leader must Know and Do. The Know and Do arenas are closely interlinked, in part because much of the learning that contributes to knowing what to do comes from doing, i.e., from experience. Under these rubrics the doctrine identifies four general categories of skills needed for successful leadership (interpersonal, conceptual, technical, and tactical skills) and three types of actions that officers must take (influencing, operating, and improving the units and systems under their command). Recent official updates (e.g., U.S. Army Training and Doctrine Command, 2001) also call out new requirements, often implying some change in the way leaders need to reason toward sound decisions. For example, it is now said that officers need "self-awareness" (roughly, understanding one's own capabilities and limitations relative to the situation) and "adaptability" (an ability to learn new things necessary in changing circumstances and change accordingly).

In this monograph we focus on more detailed abilities that fall into those general categories. In most treatments the technical and tactical dimensions of knowledge tend to be the most prominent, but we argue that those two dimensions are not sufficient by themselves. For example, to gain situational understanding—a comprehensive picture of the battle space—conceptual and interpersonal skills are as important as tactical and technical skills. Thus, while the same general attributes may be required, there are apt to be many important differences in the specifics of what officers need to Know and Do.

Something New: Adapting to the Contemporary Operating Environment

To identify the "something new," we examined challenges posed by the new operational environment and analyzed the skills and background that might better enable leaders to meet those challenges. Our analysis pointed to three key areas of skills, knowledge, and ability:

Specific operational skills. Analysis of recent and ongoing operations suggested several skill areas that now require more emphasis because they have become more important, more complex, or required at lower echelons of leadership. These skills include

- Facility in joint and combined arms operations
- Dealing with civilian populations
- Force protection
- Operations in urban or restricted terrain
- Understanding the enemy situation
- Using technology for situational awareness
- Integrating coalition forces
- Interacting with media.

Intellectual and cognitive abilities. The contemporary environment places a heightened premium on making decisions quickly, in unfamiliar situations amid greater ambiguity and uncertainty than leaders faced in the not-so-distant past. In such circumstances, leaders have to short-cut the time-consuming decision-making processes taught in school; instead they rely on less formal "recognitional" decision making, based on models from their experience.

Breadth of knowledge and perspective. While intellectual abilities are essential, they are not sufficient for effective decision making. Leaders also need a broad base of experience and background knowledge to inform their decisions, particularly in fluid and unfamiliar environments. This base includes both a tactical or operational component (exposure to a wide array of operational environments) and a broader intellectual component (knowledge and appreciation of nonmilitary and non-U.S. environments and institutions). Since officers' careers are already chock-full of demands on their time, attaining this breadth will be a challenge.

Experience: The Foundation for Leader Development

Our analysis indicates that future leaders will need more preparation and experience. How much more operational experience can leaders attain, given the time they have in a career and the many other things that officers must do? To address that question, we modeled sequences of officers' assignments and other activities during the course of their early career. We focused our modeling efforts primarily on operational experience *in units*—always the military's preferred venue for developing leaders and sharpening operational skills—but we also included time for periods of education in Army schools that parallel current professional education sequences.

In selecting people for promotion and for command positions, the military system accords heavy weight to previous operational experience, and especially to previous successful *command experience* in operational environments. Our analysis adopted that orientation and sought to determine how much leadership and operational experience leaders could be provided along their career paths. The analysis also considered experiences in non-unit organizational assignments that would enhance an officer's understanding of operations and tactics—such as a position as observer-controller at a Combat Training Center (CTC).

With these ideas in mind, we designed a model to explore the ways in which officer career paths can impart opportunities for operational experience, while still satisfying other demands (e.g., time attending professional schools or performing institutional functions). In essence, the object of the model was to assess how well the system can provide the experiential dimensions needed to produce (1) cohorts of officers who are well prepared to assume leadership positions within the grades of O-2 through O-4; and (2) a cohort of officers promoted to O-5 who are well prepared for battalion command.

We employed the model to identify feasible sets of career paths that would produce future leaders who had noticeably higher amounts of experience in operational units than in the past. For example, the model represented selection processes that would favor officers with repeated operational assignments, particularly in new or transforming units. In one case, we even stipulated that leaders would need to be considerably more senior to take on command positions—e.g., requiring that company commanders in new units always be O-4s rather than O-3s.

Overall, the results of the analysis are encouraging: the model yielded feasible solutions for every set of officer requirements we specified. The Army has latitude, therefore, to provide its leaders more time in field units and more exposure to operational challenges, if it needs to do so. Within the constraints of the current position structure, it is possible to ensure that many officers get repeated operational assignments. We also found that the Army could build significant repetitive experience in *new* (or transforming) units, even to the point of developing a cadre of officers who get multiple leadership assignments in such units.

However, creating this degree of depth in operational experience comes at the expense of breadth. While the paths we modeled would produce a group of officers with high operational expertise, those same officers would lack much exposure to the Army's TDA institutions. Moreover, another group of officers would move along different paths, which would provide them little exposure to operational assignments beyond early years of service. Similar findings also apply to the distinction regarding service in transforming units: while the system can produce some officers with solid depth in new or transforming units, such a policy would simultaneously create another group of officers with little or no experience in such units.

Because of these drawbacks, we conclude that some other actions would probably be necessary if the Army needed to pursue sharply higher levels of operational experience for many officers, especially in new or transforming units. While it is too soon to know whether or how much of this may be necessary, we suggest that the most promising course is to supplement the development of operational expertise in non-unit settings.

Supplementing Experience: Combining Venues for Leader Development

Evidently, not all required development can be accomplished through unit experience. Other venues will be needed, and for some skills those other venues may be more appropriate. We concluded that this applies particularly to two of the primary types of skills and knowledge that we identified.

Intellectual and cognitive skills for decision making. Recent years have seen renewed recognition within the Army that the modern environment calls not just for specific skills, but also for better-developed intellectual abilities. Leaders need to know how to think about novel situations and demands and how to devise a course of action fitted to those demands. They also need to know how to learn, and to become confident that they can acquire new skills and knowledge quickly when they confront new challenges. These skills and attributes underlie the key ability in operational command: the ability to make a good enough decision soon enough to count.

This set of skills and attributes includes the main attributes that support recognitional decision making:

- Pattern recognition
- Ability to gain situational understanding
- Facility with mental simulation
- Critical thinking
- Adaptability

All of the above skills are inherently *cognitive* processes (modes of thinking). Thus, they are amenable to development in an academic, institutional setting: their development calls for reflection on past experience, ferreting out the essential elements of a new problem, entertaining alternatives, and thinking through the consequences of actions that have not yet been taken. Institutional education has long-proven worth in teaching these kinds of skills, and thus it can play a key role in developing and refining the meta-competencies for operational command: the ability to develop comprehensive situational understanding and the ability to use it to produce effective solutions and decisions. Combining this intellectual grounding with the application of such skills in operational environments, using simulations or practical exercises, will help to hone both the general and the specific skills. While some of this may be accomplished in fast-paced operational environments, units' practical constraints and time limits mean that the predominant role in developing intellectual skills must be played by academic institutions. We argue that there is a role in this process both for the Army's institutional schools and for graduate civilian education.

Breadth of knowledge and perspective. Breadth is becoming more important for leaders, for two main reasons. First, as important as the above cognitive skills are, their successful application rests on a base of wide experience and knowledge. Familiarity with a wider range of possible operational situations will give an officer a wider array of knowledge on which to draw when evaluating possible courses of action. The broader the base, the greater the likelihood a leader will find a similar situation on which to base such evaluations.

Second, familiarity with external institutions and cultures (e.g., other services, Joint commands, and government agencies) aids not only in planning and conducting operations, but also in gaining support from or influencing the actions of these external players. The same need for breadth applies to familiarity with foreign institutions, both military and civilian. Recent operational experiences at all echelons of the U.S. military—in the Balkans, Afghanistan, and Iraq—have brought this point home. This kind of breadth is achievable only through contact with external institutions, and its importance argues for greater exposure of officers to graduate education and broadening assignments outside the Army.

Recommendations

We begin our recommendations by re-emphasizing the "something old": the Army should continue to acquire and develop leaders with the character traits and values that have always been the underpinning of effective leadership. Leaders who are not so grounded will fail, regardless of technical or operational skills, because their subordinates will not follow them.

Beyond that essential base of leadership, our findings imply that considerably more needs to be done to develop leaders who are well prepared to meet the challenges of the contemporary environment and to continually learn and adapt to new circumstances. To accomplish that preparation, we suggest the following avenues of approach:

- Develop more **education modules** specifically designed to develop competence and confidence in less formal, more rapid decision-making skills. These should pose both military and nonmilitary challenges.
- Develop more **practical exercise** tools that proffer a wider array of challenges, consistent with the contemporary operating environment, for use both in education modules (as above) and in field environments. The Army is already working to include more diverse challenges in its training modules at the Combat Training Centers.
- Capitalize on **distributed learning** capabilities to support predeployment (or, for that matter, postdeployment) familiarization as well as self-study programs. These tools can quickly take users through a variety of situations and thus can supplement other efforts to enhance breadth.
- Give officers **dedicated learning time**, in both academic and unit settings, to develop and broaden their skills.
- Provide greater opportunities for officers, especially those in the operations career field, to receive **advanced civil schooling.**[2] Graduate education inculcates depth in the key intellectual skills we have cited, and will also broaden perspectives in ways that other experiences cannot.
- Broaden **professional military education**. Focus more on other institutions and cultures and how to cooperate with them. Increase opportunities to study in the schools of other services and nations, possibly as a supplement to the Army's professional academic curricula. Broaden exposure by including more foreign students, civilians, and officers from other services in Army schools.

---

[2] We stress that this should be in addition to, not at the expense of, opportunities for officers in technical or other specialties that depend heavily on such education.

- Set aside some **dedicated positions** specifically for the purpose of broadening officers who would not normally be designated for such positions. Officers could be "seconded" to these positions; while their primary purpose would be to learn, they could also make a direct contribution. An example would be a combat arms officer "seconded" to a position in strategic planning; a strategic planner could also be "seconded" as a deputy operations officer in a Joint command.
- **Lengthen careers.** Most of the alternatives above become more feasible if officers have more time to spend in each assignment and at each level. The current array of key developmental "gates" is so extensive as to be almost exclusively prescriptive. Adding additional developmental requirements (like "seconding" or more schooling) without adding more time would further complicate this situation.
- Access and develop a **larger inventory of officers**. This could go hand in hand with longer careers. Like longer careers, this would require major changes and resource investments, and thus would require a long-term planning horizon. However, it seems likely that many of the initiatives suggested above could be taken only with a larger base of officers to work with. We argue that while the current grade pyramid may have been suitable when it was designed, it may not allow enough officers to meet all the requirements of the modern environment. At a minimum, the overall specifications for inventory and structure should be reviewed to assess whether they can meet modern requirements for breadth and depth.

The challenges we have laid out are significant, but not insurmountable. The Army excels at developing the detailed listings of tasks and subtasks that would comprise the skills we have enumerated, along with a collection of supporting exercise and simulation vignettes. Some steps in this direction have already been taken. But implementing the ideas contained here—or others that grow out of them—will take time and money. It will be harder still to bring about the changes needed to better develop intellectual skills and broaden perspectives. This points up a need for more investments in schooling, more time for development during a career, and perhaps more officers in the force. Nevertheless, we argue that investments along these lines will be needed if the Army is to meet its responsibilities as a profession, which include the development of new officers and the maintenance of the body of expertise essential for military functions in the future.

Acknowledgments

The list of people to whom we are indebted for contributions to this project would easily fill more than one page. At the risk of slighting some, we choose to mention a few. LTG Larry Jordan, the TRADOC Chief of Staff at the inception of this project, was a major impetus; he encouraged us to share his wide perspective. BG (then COL) Joe Martz, then Commander of the Operations Group at the National Training Center, was similarly inclined as an operational thinker and trainer, and he helped us get the best of insights and thinking from his extraordinarily talented group of combat trainers. We learned much from our resident Army Fellows, MAJ(P) Caron Wilbur, LTC Gary D. Quintero, and LTC L. Jerome Campbell, who also contributed greatly to our scenario analysis. Our colleagues Jerry Bracken and Richard Darilek reviewed an earlier draft of this document, providing thoughtful comments and insights that led to significant improvements in our presentation. Finally, none of our work would have been possible without the unswerving support of Gordon Rogers, who coordinated our travel and our interactions with the TRADOC staff, assembled references for us, and continually gave us advice and friendship.

Glossary

ACR	Armored Cavalry Regiment
ARTEP	Army Training and Evaluation Program
ATLDP	Army Training and Leader Development Panel
BOS	Battlefield Operating System
CDR	Commander
COE	Contemporary Operating Environment
CTC	Combat Training Center
DL	Distributed Learning (also Distance Learning)
ENH	TDA position that enhances operational/warfighting skills
INST	TDA institutional position
LDR	Leader in a TOE unit
MDMP	Military Decision-Making Process
MRE	Mission Readiness Exercise (also Mission Rehearsal Exercise, sometimes abbreviated MRX)
NATO	North Atlantic Treaty Organization
NGO	Nongovernmental Organization
OCOKA	Mnemonic acronym for "Observation, Cover and concealment, Obstacles, Key terrain, Avenues of approach"
OPFOR	Opposing Force, typically those forces arrayed against forces being trained at the CTCs
PL	Platoon Leader
PMAD	Personnel Manning Authorization Document
RC	Reserve Component(s)
ROE	Rules of Engagement
ROK	Republic of Korea (South Korea)
ROTC	Reserve Officers' Training Corps

S1	Personnel management officer (aka adjutant), typically for a battalion or a brigade-level staff
S3	Operations officer, again typically battalion or brigade staff
S4	Supply officer on battalion or brigade staff
STX	Situational Training Exercise
TDA	Table of Distribution and Allowances; also a descriptor for organizations with institutional responsibilities. Contrast with TOE, below.
TOE	Table of Organization and Equipment; also a descriptor for units typically found in the Army's operational forces.
WMD	Weapon(s) of Mass Destruction
XO	Executive Officer

CHAPTER ONE

Introduction

Background

The past 15 years have seen profound changes in the missions and environments for U.S. military operations, with the potential for equally profound effects on the things that Army leaders must know and do. What we now call the "contemporary operating environment" began to emerge with the collapse of the Soviet Union, which had been the focus of war planning for nearly 50 years. Although some features of the new environment had appeared in earlier contingency planning, they now took center stage in a series of sharply different operations set in unfamiliar locations—such as Somalia, Bosnia, Kosovo, and Haiti, punctuated by the first Gulf War. Then came the onset of international terrorism directed at the United States, culminating in the attacks of September 2001 and followed by the conflicts in Afghanistan and Iraq. Simultaneously, underlying all of this has been the steady progress of globalization, making it easier for anyone—including U.S. adversaries and terrorists—to move quickly among nations, to acquire and distribute information, weapons, and other technologies, and to involve civilian populations in war, either directly or vicariously.

These changes have created a dynamic situation—volatile, unpredictable, and novel in many respects. For military planners and leaders, the face of war is certainly more complex and varied than at any time in memory. Future missions are uncertain and current ones complex; opponents may change quickly; fighting takes place on terrain that differs from training grounds, under conditions that were not envisioned; and perhaps most important, the presence of civilians is a much more salient and pervasive factor than ever before. Of course, the Department of Defense and the Army recognized these changing conditions and had taken some steps to adapt to them even during the Cold War. But the momentum for adaptation and change began gathering in earnest in the decade after the Soviet collapse. More and more during this time, publications in military circles contain phrases pertaining to new operational circumstances: for example, they speak of a nonlinear battlefield, shifting coalitions, diverse cultural environments, increased operational tempo, the importance of information dominance, and the need for all military services to interact with joint, multinational, and civilian systems.

The official response to the evolving environment, however, has centered largely on the tangible elements and mechanics of war: weapons, logistics, unit organization, and basing.[1] Not as much attention was paid at first to how the contemporary environment affects soldiers and especially *leaders*. For example, transformation in the Army has been primarily concerned with power projection, the need for lighter and more mobile vehicles, and the conduct of information operations. Leader preparation and "people" issues in general do appear in briefings and papers, but, until relatively recently, without much specificity. Nevertheless, it seems possible that the new environment may call for different skills, greater knowledge in certain areas, or a different intellectual orientation toward command and decision making. And so we asked: Have recent changes in the operational environment affected leadership requirements? And if so, should corresponding changes be made in how officers are educated, developed, and prepared for their future missions?

Focus and Content of This Report

This document reports the results of a research project that addressed those questions. It took place within a context in which some official concern about officer development was already evident.[2] For example, in the late 1990s the Army revised its Officer Personnel Management System, altering the career paths available to field-grade officers. These changes were in part a response to the need to develop an officer corps with greater degrees of sophistication in many different skill areas so that officers would be better able to cope with advances in technology and the increased complexity of operations. Accordingly, the changes were designed to allow a greater degree of specialization within the officer corps and thus to increase an officer's depth of skills within his or her chosen field.[3]

More recently, the Army undertook an introspective look at how it could ensure that officers are ready for the fluidity of the contemporary environment. The answer was framed in terms of quite general attributes: officers were said to need "self-awareness" (roughly, understanding one's own capabilities and limitations relative to

---

[1] Both DoD and the Army have undertaken various efforts at transformation to adapt to the new circumstances (Office of the Secretary of Defense, 2003; Department of the Army, 2003). The United States is also taking steps to shed some of its Cold War–era overseas bases and adopt a basing posture that is aligned more closely with military requirements of the new era (Gilmore, 2004). There has also been much attention paid to the effects of frequent deployments and "high tempo" on soldiers in the aggregate (see Sortor and Polich, 2001). However, this concern has not been matched by analysis of how leaders are affected.

[2] Parallel concerns may apply to noncommissioned officers and other leaders, such as Army civilians and even contractor personnel. However, we limited our scope to commissioned officers.

[3] For details of these changes and their rationale, see OPMS XXI Task Force (1997).

the situation) and "adaptability" (an ability to learn new things made necessary by changing circumstances and to change accordingly).[4]

We felt, however, that more specificity was needed. Although the time seems ripe for a wide-ranging re-examination of leader development, we found no analytically oriented assessment of how things have changed and how such changes might affect requirements for leaders. This report supplies an assessment of that sort, aimed at two main issues: First, what altered features of the operational environment imply new challenges for Army leaders, and what form do the challenges take? Second, what skills and background should leaders develop to meet those challenges? We also comment upon the pros and cons of various ways in which the Army might foster that development.

This report will argue that the contemporary operating environment calls for three classes of skills and background that need greater attention than they have been accorded in the past:

- General intellectual and cognitive skills to support more rapid and adaptive decision making, prompted by the volatility and unfamiliarity of contemporary conditions;
- Specific operational skills suited to the new environment; and
- Greater breadth of perspective and knowledge, including nonmilitary and non-U.S. cultural awareness.

Chapter Two deals with the first item above. It examines the enduring foundations of military leadership ("something old"), explores the general attributes that leaders need, and discusses how requirements for some of those attributes have evolved in recent years (a beginning for discussion of "something new"). Chapter Three studies the specific aspects of environments where military operations have recently occurred or may be expected to occur. It derives an analytic description of the features of the new environment and ties those features to specific operational skills that leaders need to have. Chapter Four uses a quantitative model to explore how the Army could increase officers' time in operational assignments—the key venue in which such skills have traditionally been developed. Chapter Five discusses the subject from the opposite perspective, considering the need for officer *breadth* as well as operational depth. Finally, Chapter Six ties all of these findings together into a set of conclusions and recommendations.

---

[4] U.S. Army Training and Doctrine Command, Army Training and Leader Development Panel (2001).

Sources and Methods

Our approach to these questions depended on three main sources of information and data. First, we gained general perspectives by reviewing the Army's own doctrinal publications on military leadership. We also reviewed prominent recent studies concerned with how military leadership is changing[5] and how the contemporary environment is evolving.[6] In addition, we attended numerous Army conferences and staff discussions on officer leadership and officer personnel management, covering a wide variety of viewpoints.

To supplement this, as our ideas developed, we conducted approximately 40 interviews with experts in military doctrine, officers serving in operational units, and academic personnel involved in teaching officers at Army schools. To support detailed analysis of recent operational environments, we drew upon the real-world experience of Army officers who were recently assigned to RAND and had participated in one or more operations since 1990. Finally, to facilitate quantitative analysis of officer careers, we obtained and analyzed data describing all officer positions in the U.S. Army. We relied on these sources to paint a picture of the challenges that officers now face and how leader development practices can help future officers to meet those challenges.

---

[5] See Chapter Two for details. These studies included analysis by the Army Training and Leader Development Panel, curriculum redesign studies conducted for the Training and Doctrine Command, and work on officer professionalism by scholars at the U.S. Military Academy.

[6] See Chapter Three for details. The primary intellectual impetus for examination of the "contemporary operating environment" came from the Army's Training and Doctrine Command, but the resulting ideas have gained much wider currency.

CHAPTER TWO

Military Leadership: From the General to the Specific

In this chapter we will describe how we sorted through a wide array of leadership constructs and important leader attributes and decided to focus analysis on a subset of requirements that appear particularly challenging in the modern environment. We begin with an overview of Army leadership concepts, as represented in doctrinal publications and Army traditions. These concepts reflect the service's established formulation of key attributes—aspects of character, knowledge, and ability—needed for effective leadership. They are based on long experience, adapted over many years to represent fundamental qualities that officers and leaders should have, year in and year out, in any environment. As such, these concepts are necessarily oriented to more or less stable requirements. Many of these traits have roots that go back long before modern times; indeed, the character attributes and values we outline below are as old as leadership itself.

These enduring attributes of leadership remain important. However, the recent past has been anything but stable, in terms of situations and missions facing U.S. armed forces. Emerging trends suggest that it may be time to review the inventory of skills and experiences given to officers in preparation for leadership positions. In fact, a number of recent publications by observers inside and outside the Army have begun to grapple with these changes, suggesting intellectual leadership abilities that may need more emphasis in the future. Accordingly, in the second section of this chapter we outline some of these recent perspectives and relate them to one another and to the Army's concept.

Finally, in the third section of this chapter we present our own viewpoint and synthesis, focusing on key skills and attributes that we think leaders need as they confront today's more fluid environment. This synthesis is a precursor for more detailed discussions in subsequent chapters; it outlines a general model of how leaders respond and adapt their own thinking as they confront new situations. It places a heavy premium on having a *range of experience* to draw upon, as well as having key *intellectual attributes* (such as flexibility and critical thinking skills) that facilitate rapid and well-informed decision making. We will argue that in the contemporary environment, leaders increasingly need not only the time-honored general attributes, but also broader experience and a more highly developed ability to make rapid decisions based on that experience.[1] The challenge is to continue to impart the general leadership attributes and at the same time to develop differently—more thoroughly, more comprehensively, and more quickly—the subset of skills and experience required in the emerging environment.

The Army Construct: Be–Know–Do

The Army has long recognized that military leaders must have both the general attributes that are common to leadership in a wide variety of fields, and an array of operational, tactical, and technical skills that are uniquely military in nature. Since almost all operational leaders acquire both the general and the military-unique skills during their military careers, the career progression system must develop both of them.[2] Naturally there is an extensive literature on leadership and its particular features in a military environment.[3] Although we did not attempt to survey all of this work, we draw from a selected portion of it to describe briefly the range, number, and diversity of skills and attributes to which this literature refers.

An appropriate starting point is the Army's long-standing formulation, built around three aspects of a leader that are considered critical:

- What the leader must *Be* (the persona, primarily but not exclusively oriented on character);
- What he or she must *Know* (from very general to very specific areas of knowledge and skill, over a range of disciplines); and
- What he or she must *Do* (the kinds of actions leaders must take to make their organizations accomplish their tasks and function effectively).

---

[1] This special ability is known as "recognitional" decision making (Klein, 1998), in which a central role is played by recognizing how a new situation resembles situations previously encountered. This implies an experience base, but recognition can also include analogies or patterns learned otherwise. As we discuss later in this chapter, this process also involves several other high-level skills, all of which take time to develop.

[2] Although the military taps external sources for leaders in some specialized functions (such as medical and legal professionals), the core military functions have almost exclusively required leaders who have been developed in the Army environment.

[3] A search of the catalog of the Library of Congress, for example, produced more than 1,500 titles containing "leadership." See Fielder (1994) and Leed (2002) for a review of the relevant academic literature. The Army, of course, has its own extensive doctrinal literature; see, for example, the material in Field Manual 22-100 (Department of the Army, *Army Leadership*, 1999, and its new draft version, FM 6-22), and the other documents cited there.

Persona: What the Leader Should "Be"

Leadership, in this account, is fundamentally the act or process of influencing others to accomplish what the leader wants to accomplish (or, as a slight variant, to behave in ways in which the leader wants them to behave). Leaders influence people to accomplish and behave by providing them with purpose, direction, and motivation.[4] The Army's doctrine, in common with other treatments of leadership, particularly emphasizes character as an essential foundation for providing purpose, direction, and motivation to others. For example, the early sections of the Army's premier leadership manual, FM 22-100, concentrate almost exclusively on the key human qualities, character, and values the Army seeks in leaders. We say "almost exclusively" because these chapters do mention the need for more specific abilities such as critical thinking,[5] communication, and tactical and technical skills, but largely in the context of their contribution to the complete leader persona.

What are these core values and attributes? The doctrine lists seven values that form the essence of military character: loyalty, duty, respect, selfless service, honor, integrity, and personal courage. Other attributes that fill out the leader persona fall into three categories: mental, physical, and emotional. The mental category includes will, self-discipline, initiative, judgment, self-confidence, intelligence, and cultural awareness. The physical dimension includes health fitness, more narrowly defined physical fitness, and military and professional bearing. The most important emotional attributes are identified as self-control, balance, and stability.[6]

Historical support for this concept of character can be found in a 1984 study of past combat leaders, compiled by the U.S. Military Academy's Department of History.[7] That paper was prepared as part of a review examining the Army's officer personnel management system, aimed at identifying key attributes that the system should help to preserve and develop. Noting that "successful leadership in combat should be the aim of the system used to manage officers' careers in any army," the authors presented a tour of successes and failures in combat leadership and inferred some common characteristics of successful leaders. Prominent among those common

---

[4] This phrasing, with minor variants, appears in numerous places (e.g., FM 22-100, p. 2-11; Department of the Army, Pamphlet 350-58, 1994, p. 2). In what appears to be the precursor of this formulation, an earlier one provided by Wass de Czege (1986) includes *continuity*; in that view, the leader looks not only to the accomplishment of immediate objectives but also to the sustainment, refinement, and, if necessary, renewal of the organization's ability to meet the challenges of the future. Note that the leader must also be able to discern the proper mix of purpose, direction, motivation, and continuity appropriate for each situation. This will not always be obvious.

[5] Critical thinking, or in the Army's parlance "critical reasoning," is a term used to cover a variety of evaluative mental processes. A cogent definition (from Cohen, Freeman, and Thompson, 2000) describes it as the process of positing an explanation or hypothesis (a "story" that purports to account for an observation), testing the story against available evidence, and adjusting the story in response.

[6] FM 22-100, pp. 2-6 through 2-39 and 2-67 through 2-79.

[7] Hamburger (1984).

characteristics were some of the same character attributes outlined above (albeit in somewhat different words), including:

- Unquestioned integrity (cited by the study as the "*sine qua non*");
- Control of self, situation, and unit ("balanced, imperturbable");
- Moral courage;
- Positive self-image, enhanced usually by fitness and good health.

Thus, the leader character traits observed historically are similar to those called for in the doctrine.

Knowledge and Skill: What the Leader Should "Know" and "Do"

The second major element of the Army's leadership construct is what the leader must Know. Under this rubric the doctrine identifies four general categories of skills needed for successful leadership: interpersonal, conceptual, technical, and tactical skills. Later in this chapter and more heavily in Chapter Three, we will focus on more detailed abilities that fall into these general categories. In most discussions—including ours—the technical and tactical dimensions tend to appear somewhat more frequently. However, we caution against inferring that those two dimensions are sufficient by themselves. As we will argue later, to achieve "situational understanding"—a comprehensive picture of the battle space—conceptual and interpersonal skills are as important as tactical and technical skills.

The doctrine's third element, Do, covers actions that leaders take: influencing, operating, and improving the units and systems under their command. In Chapter Three we will elaborate on emerging requirements for actions that fit all three of these categories, but primarily in the areas of influencing (decision making in particular) and operating (both planning and execution). Because leaders must first know how to do things before they can take effective action, our examination in that chapter will concentrate more on the Know and less on the Be and the Do. However, the Know and Do arenas are closely interlinked, in part because much of the learning that contributes to knowing what to do comes from doing, i.e., from experience. In fact, the U.S. military has always placed high value on operational experience, time in operational units, and previous command experience as the hallmarks of a leader who knows what to do.

Other Perspectives on Leadership

Military Professionalism

A second perspective that merits comment results from a resurgence of discussions of military professionalism, sometimes rendered—perhaps too narrowly—as "officership." For example, when the Army recently conducted a re-examination of training and leader development (the Army Training and Leader Development Panel, ATLDP), several issues relating to professionalism occupied a prominent place in the findings. In particular, in the process of considering core competencies, the ATLDP urged a re-emphasis on military professionalism and recommended that the Army:

- Define and teach officership and an Army service ethic;
- Develop, publish, and maintain commissioned officer performance standards;
- Emphasize lifelong learning as a responsibility shared by the Army and its professionals.[8]

Similar concerns about professionalism and officership have been voiced by several other authors, appearing prominently in academic discussions. But what does it mean to be a "military professional"? Snider (2003)[9] cites four essential aspects of officership:

- Warfighter;
- Servant to the nation;
- Member of the Army profession;
- Leader of character.

In keeping with other discussions of professionalism, this formulation tends to concentrate on broad aspects of the leader's role, such as professional ethics and the warrior ethos. These broad aspects are generally interpreted as subsuming the leader traits called out in FM 22-100. For example, "leader of character" calls to mind the values and character traits of FM 22-100. "Servant to the nation" recalls the values of loyalty and selfless service. "Warfighter" subsumes the knowledge and skills that appear under the Army's "Know" rubric, as does "member of the Army profession." Note also that these aspects run closely parallel with the traits enumerated in the Military Academy's study (Hamburger, 1984). Thus, conceived of as aspects of professional identity, the four taken together provide a picture generally similar to the "Be-Know-Do" paradigm.

Military professionalism, however, implies broader responsibilities than these lists of traits may suggest. There is an extensive academic literature underlying Snider's four points (Matthews, Snider, and Watkins, 2002). Briefly abstracting from this literature, we see four key attributes of a profession; these also help to explain why this construct is now receiving increased attention:

---

[8] U.S. Army Training and Doctrine Command, Army Training and Leader Development Panel (2001).

[9] This material was presented to an Army Officership Doctrinal Integration Conference in 2003. The conference was partly a response to the ATLDP's call for developing a unified concept of "officership" (or military professionalism).

- **Expertise and knowledge.** Professionals such as physicians and attorneys are expected to master an abstract body of knowledge and to apply it effectively to manage their clients' problems. As Snider writes, "professions excel . . . *in the creation, adaptation, and application of abstract expert knowledge to new situations.*" (Emphasis added.)
- **Trust and legitimacy.** The client, or society at large, recognizes and values the professional's special expertise. Thus, people turn to physicians to solve medical problems and to lawyers to handle litigation and criminal matters. Likewise the clergy enjoy special status and authority in dealing with religious and ethical matters.[10] Note that the assignment of trust connects closely with the character foundation.
- **Autonomy.** A profession enjoys considerable autonomy in key functions, such as codifying a body of knowledge, inculcating it in new members, enforcing ethics, and assessing the quality of professional practice. This autonomy grows out of the profession's specialized expertise—often impenetrable to the layman—and society's trust in the profession to "do the right thing" even when the client cannot be certain what the right thing would be.
- **Jurisdiction.** A profession exercises decisive control over venues and activities that constitute its focus: hospitals, courtrooms, churches, etc. Moreover, these areas are of grave importance—they "really matter"—to clients and society (e.g., matters of personal health, community justice, and religious faith). Jurisdiction is tied to autonomy and legitimacy, of course; with autonomous jurisdiction comes responsibility, and successful execution of responsibility is the foundation for future legitimacy.

It can readily be seen how these four attributes can apply to the military as a profession. An Army officer must master a body of specialized expertise in operations and strategic thinking. The military enjoys legitimacy because of its central role—and past success—in defending the nation's security and vital interests. In part because of this legitimacy, the military is granted considerable autonomy in its operations by other agencies of government (e.g., the courts) and by society at large. And at least during wartime, the military controls the battlefield and a vast support and industrial structure, over which its jurisdiction is taken for granted.

Nevertheless, these attributes are not as firmly established in the military case as they may be in the case of "civilian" professionals. We suspect that explains the apparent increase of concern within the military about its professional status. Two con-

---

[10] Burk (2002) discusses how the standing of various professions has varied over the past several centuries as the public's view of what is credible knowledge has shifted from religious or spiritual sources toward scientific evidence.

cerns in particular warrant notice, because they are related to the changing environment that may challenge future leaders and thus relevant to our discussions of leader development requirements. First, several observers perceive *"competition for control"* of the military jurisdiction (Snider and Watkins, 2002; Burk, 2002). They note that the domains for military operations have progressively expanded over the past century. Once their domain was primarily fighting on the battlefield. In the 20th century that expanded to managing a much larger defense function—what we might term "the military component of the nation's comprehensive security strategy." More recently, as Burk says, the military has been called upon to manage "peace" (e.g., by separating warring parties and restoring stability) and even to manage the welfare of people in foreign nations (e.g., humanitarian operations). Thus officers are involved in actions extending beyond the realm that many would consider "typically military." Naturally there are other actors who also claim expertise in these domains—such as other agencies of government, humanitarian organizations, and international bodies. That complicates matters for the officer corps, adding new domains of knowledge and practice that must be mastered for the officer to maintain a self-perception as a competent professional.

Second, the new circumstances create challenges in the key function of maintenance and renewal of the profession. This function is likely to become especially important under circumstances calling for more, not less, diversity in the education, skill, and experiences of the profession's members.[11] We suggest that in the current environment, military professional institutions need to cover a wider scope of knowledge, impart that knowledge both to novices and to established practitioners, rearticulate ethical principles as they apply to novel situations, and represent the profession to outsiders who may question its relevance to current problems. Of course, that is an important goal for Army schools—but the tension between goals and resources (particularly students' time available) makes it more difficult now than in previous eras.

Skills Needed for a Changing Environment

The past few years have seen a number of attempts at formulating alternative leadership concepts, responding in part to a sense that current events present new challenges for officers and the Army development system. Most of these recognize a need for leaders to adapt in response to the new environment, but they also try to place the need in the context of very general attributes or skills. In discussing the derivations of these traits over the next few paragraphs, we will relate them to the fundamental "Be-Know-Do" construct and show how they point toward aspects of leader development that need more emphasis. We will provide an example that suggests more specific

---

[11] Snider and Watkins (2002) emphasize this also.

leader characteristics, discuss some important ATLDP findings, and point out ways in which both efforts provide perspectives on our subsequent treatments of leader qualities.

Some recent work done by Cubic, Inc. for the Army Command and General Staff College (CGSC) undertook to identify highly specific areas of knowledge, intellectual skills, and traits needed by field-grade officers, with a view toward helping the Army map out curriculum requirements for its CGSC courses.[12] This resulted in a wide-ranging list of intellectual, tactical, and technical skills needed for success as a mid-level commander or staff officer, positions typically held by field-grade officers.

For example, one of the Cubic reports lists "what the leader is": adaptive, self-aware, competent, a critical thinker, oriented toward life-long learning, and "a leader of character with the warrior ethos." Then, translating into more specific terms, the report also lists "what the leader will be":

- A battalion commander who masters leadership, visualization, and specialty skills;
- A staff expert in operational and institutional positions (at levels from battalion up);
- A leader serving both the field Army and the institutional Army;
- A graduate-level warfighter and technical specialist.

Cubic's general description of what the leader should Be closely matches the Army's in its reference to the values and character foundations. But the above list also covers by implication many of the Know and Do aspects: to be the things on the list above, the leader must perforce know and be able to do many things that involve technical, tactical, and interpersonal skills. Along these lines, the Cubic effort went beyond the above catalog and sought to determine what that leader should learn as preparation for his or her position. Because this effort was pointed toward revising the Command and General Staff College curriculum, it needed to identify more specific areas in which leaders should be knowledgeable—i.e., to reinforce (or reorient) the knowledge dimension of leadership. Therefore the study explored competencies that officers should possess in order to achieve key goals emphasized in Army publications, such as shaping complex Army and joint operations, overcoming "friction and fog," dominating the full-spectrum environment, and achieving "operational overmatch." In the process, the study identified a large set of specific competencies and supporting skills conceived as necessary to operate in the modern environment. The set was quite wide-ranging and challenging. For example, among many other things, the report calls for abilities to deal with:

---

[12] Cubic Defense Applications Group (2003).

- Nonlinear battlefields;
- Fluid change with force participants, resulting in revolving coalitions and partners;
- Diverse cultural demographic and physical environments;
- Multiple simultaneous operations;
- Asymmetrical threats;
- Accelerated informational and operational tempo;
- Mixing combined forces representing conventional forces, unconventional forces, and interagency elements widely dispersed as small mobile combat teams;
- Emerging technical systems that promise information dominance (i.e., the growing array of technically sophisticated digital systems for collecting and disseminating information, exercising command and control, and supporting decision making);
- Interacting Army, joint, multinational, and civilian systems.

Besides refining our understanding of the knowledge dimension, reviewing the Cubic list yields hints of several important trends, on which we will elaborate in Chapter Three: a wider variety of operation types (a "full spectrum" from major conflict to peacekeeping); emergence of novel threats (such as unconventional weapons and suicide attacks); and the increasing importance of combined arms and joint capabilities (systems that provide "combat multipliers," with implications that permeate all echelons down to the platoon level).

Although focused on specific skills and qualities, Cubic's exposition resembled the ATLDP in its emphasis on general "meta-competencies." The ATLDP perceived a challenge arising from the fluid circumstances that officers face in the contemporary environment—a panoply of differing situations and potential adversaries. How, it was asked, can the Army ensure that its officers are ready for this variability and unpredictability? The proffered response was to identify two key competencies—*self-awareness* and *adaptability*—that stand above others as enduring intellectual attributes of the individual. These were referred to as "meta-competencies," overarching traits that make it possible to use the more specific skills needed in the contemporary and future operating environments.

These terms have taken on considerable currency in the Army, and they will figure later in our synthesis of key skills, so let us briefly clarify their various connotations. Self-awareness is the understanding of one's own capabilities, knowledge, skills, and limitations, and "knowing enough to know when you don't know enough" and must seek to learn more. Self-awareness is necessary, according to this formulation, so that leaders can recognize when things have changed and when one needs new information, skills, or resources. Consistent with this concept, we would suggest that in the context of commanding operational forces, "self-awareness" would extend to a comprehension of the capabilities and condition of those forces. It then ties to "situational awareness and understanding," which we will deal with presently.

Adaptability, along with related terms such as flexibility, refers to one's capacity to recognize changes in circumstances, learn what is needed to be effective in the new circumstances, and modify behavior accordingly. Flexibility is the capacity to make the changes as needed and soon enough: reallocate resources, redirect activities, and cause other units to make needed adjustments.[13] Adaptability has also been characterized as the "ability to understand context and to recognize and seize opportunities" and the "ability to look at a problem or crisis and see an array of unconventional solutions."[14] Taken together, these concepts expand a good deal on the knowledge dimension, especially in the sense that leaders must not only know a wide range of technical and tactical things, but also be able to synthesize the collective parts of their knowledge and adapt their thinking to unusual or unforeseen circumstances. This suggests leader development should include a hierarchy of skills and knowledge, an idea we will develop more fully later in this report.

Of course, these general ideas are not novel, nor is this the first time they have risen to importance in Army concepts of battlefield conditions and decision making. A classic example from history is the compendium *Infantry in Battle*, a compilation of vignettes from experiences of the U.S. Army and other participants in World War I.[15] The purpose of this collection was to broaden perspectives on combat decision making and to help future leaders understand the limitations of theoretical indoctrination and the value of being able to think through circumstances and apply innovative solutions. It is replete with examples in which innovation and critical thinking were lacking; most of these stories of course ended badly. George Marshall, then a colonel, wrote in the introduction, "officers who have received the best peacetime training available find themselves surprised and confused by the difference between conditions as pictured in map problems and those they encounter in campaign."[16] He went on to observe that leaders must be prepared to deal with changes and unexpected difficulties, and conditioned so their "mental processes are not paralyzed" when confronted with the unusual. Similarly, the opening subtitle of the first chapter ("Rules") is illustrative: "Combat situations cannot be solved by rule." Numerous

---

[13] This reflects our interpretation from discussions of these terms found in the Army field manuals FM 22-100, *Army Leadership* (1999) and FM 7-0, *Training the Force* (2002), as well as the ATLDP report.

[14] See, for example, Bennis and Thomas (2002), pp. 92 and 101.

[15] The Army Infantry Journal Incorporated, *Infantry in Battle* (1939).

[16] George C. Marshall, introduction to *Infantry in Battle* (1939), p. vii.

other historical treatises and memoirs consistently bring out the value of these supporting skills for adaptation.[17]

So these capabilities have been recognized for a very long time. What *is* new is the Army's re-establishment of adaptation and related traits as a central desideratum in the operational leader, which contrasts with the emphasis on the more cognitive aspects of technical and tactical/operational expertise that predominated during the Cold War period.

These recent treatments of leadership concepts illustrate two key points. First, it is possible to weave together many of the constructs of leadership, officership, and professionalism and tie them back to the Army's own foundational construct. In other words, many observers are describing similar attributes but in varying terms; this seems particularly true when looking at the traditional and enduring leader traits. But second, there is also a growing concern that the scope and complexity of attributes needed for leadership is expanding, posing problems not only for individual officers but also for the military profession as a whole. The precise nature of this expansion may be unclear, but the concern about it is palpable.

The Structure Above the Foundation: Skills for Operational Command

Focus on Decision Making in Battle Command

We turn now toward developing our own picture of those aspects of military leadership that need increased emphasis in today's more variable environment. Our formulation begins by focusing on a key function of military leaders: *decision making in battle command*.[18] This function often arose in our interviews with senior leaders and academics. Virtually all such discussions highlighted, as an essential quality, the leader's ability to execute operational decision-making responsibilities, either in combat or in a widening spectrum of situations fraught with danger and uncertainty but not necessarily involving combat per se. We sum up this skill as

The ability to make and communicate a good enough decision, soon enough to matter.

---

[17] A comprehensive treatment can be found in Doubler (1994), a detailed and carefully documented account of how the U.S. Army adapted to the enemy and circumstances it faced in the battle for Europe. Rommel (1987) and von Mellenthin (1985), among others, provide a parallel perspective from the other side of World War II. Further sources include other personal memoirs and the official histories of wars as perceived by various sides.

[18] Or, more generally, we offer the term "operational command," which we would use broadly to include the command of military forces engaged in activities not involving combat. We also recognize that leaders must perform many other functions, particularly as they reach more senior levels and become responsible for large institutions (such as national planning staffs, training facilities, or weapons acquisition programs) and highly differentiated formations (such as corps, joint commands, or multinational organizations). However, for most leaders—who are necessarily field- or company-grade officers—the most daunting challenges arise in operational command situations.

That is the essence of battle command; we argue it is the essence of command in operations other than war as well, although the circumstances may in some ways be less trying and the decision processes less time-sensitive. It is also the essence of the staff work that supports command: for the staff officer, one can simply substitute "recommendation" for "decision" in the phrase above; moreover, staff officers frequently make decisions within their purview. Regardless of the position of the leader, the exercise of this aspect of leadership is an interactive process—often truncated by time pressures—among the leader, the led, and the surrounding circumstances.

We argue that this ability has become more critical because of changes in the environment that affect fundamental aspects of battle command. We examine three aspects in which the environment could require changes in leader abilities: the overall importance, complexity, or the level at which the ability might be needed.[19] In recent and ongoing operations, many leaders have found themselves in this spot: battle command is being transformed into a more complex and faster-paced problem. Moreover, requirements for these more complex skills are migrating to lower echelons and therefore affecting more junior officers at earlier points in their careers. Because of such changes, leaders need more facility in acquiring and interpreting information, building a picture of the situation, adapting their previous plans, making decisions about how to proceed, and conveying those decisions and their rationale to their partners and subordinates.

What skills and abilities do leaders need to make good enough decisions soon enough to matter, and communicate those decisions clearly enough for subordinates to execute them as intended? To address that question, one needs a view or model of the decision-making process. Below we discuss two relevant models. First, there is a deliberate method (the Army version of which is called the "Military Decision-Making Process"), which is encouraged when circumstances permit. Second, we describe an abbreviated method—"recognitional" decision making—which seems to correspond more closely to the way that actual decision makers proceed under conditions of risk and time pressure. We will argue that in many circumstances today, more often than in the past, the leader must adopt the recognitional method. We will argue further that contemporary circumstances will frequently complicate the decision process. Thus, this method imposes demands for greater experience and more highly developed intellectual skills.

Models of Decision Making

Formal Military Decision-Making Process. Given the central importance of decision processes, a key objective of a military leader development program should be to inculcate and refine the leader's decision-making ability. The Army, to be sure, has

---

[19] Chapter Three will discuss the specific nature of these changes in much greater detail.

an elaborate and refined decision-making model, the Military Decision-Making Process (MDMP).[20] The MDMP consists of several steps that cover analysis of relevant situational factors (key among them enemy forces, weather, terrain, amount and disposition of own forces, time available) in the context of the assigned mission (which is itself carefully analyzed for its explicit tasks, implications, and constraints). The process continues with the development of alternatives (courses of action) for accomplishing the mission, evaluative comparison of the alternatives, and the recommendation of a selected alternative for the commander's decision. Staffs and commanders are expected to be well versed in the intricacies of the MDMP. The Army's professional education courses teach and review it, and training exercises have long reinforced its application. Under ideal circumstances, including the availability of sufficient information to permit good analysis and sufficient time to work through all the steps, the process has many strengths to commend it.

The problem is that under the circumstances of real operations—combat or otherwise—there is often neither sufficient information nor sufficient time to make the process work effectively. This is not a new problem; the Army has recognized it and emphasized that battle command often requires making decisions without the benefit of a completed MDMP.[21] That point is likely to grow in importance as the U.S. armed forces emphasize more rapid maneuver and more rapid adaptation to a fluid battlefield.[22]

Discussion along the lines above frequently leads to a concern that was voiced in some interviews with military experts: the Army might depart too much from its MDMP. Many worried that it would neither be taught thoroughly enough in academic environments nor practiced sufficiently in training exercises. The consensus seems to be that the MDMP is an important tool that staffs and commanders must understand, a disciplined way of thinking through military decisions that, once understood, can be abbreviated and truncated as necessary. Part of this discipline, we were told repeatedly, is the ability to distinguish between prudent and imprudent risks and to avoid too much emphasis on rapid decisions. As one expert phrased it, "sometimes deliberate is better." We note, in this context, that a decision to use more deliberate decision support processes is again a decision that needs to be good enough, and made soon enough to matter. And it will probably not be a deliberate decision in its own right.

Recognitional Decision Making. Despite such concerns, let us grant that the exigencies of real-world operations will often require decision making in less than ideal circumstances, in which neither time nor information permit deliberation. We have

---

[20] Department of the Army, *Staff Organization and Operations,* FM 101-5 (1997).

[21] Again, *Infantry in Battle* provides useful historical perspective on this point.

[22] Those assumptions are now a staple of defense planning. See U.S. Joint Staff, *Joint Vision 2020* (2000).

termed this form of decision making "recognitional," following Klein (1998), although it is sometimes described alternatively as "intuitive," "heuristic," or "naturalistic."[23] Klein cites extensive empirical evidence on processes used by real-world decision makers, all of which exemplify recognitional decision making. This formulation includes several key aspects that are relevant to our problem:[24]

- **Pattern recognition.** Recognitional decision making depends on perceptual skills such as pattern recognition: reviewing past events and situations and seeking one that serves as a "model" for the current problem. Learning this takes time and "many cases to develop."
- **Mental simulation.** To assess likely outcomes of an action, skilled decision makers can simulate events, processes, and sequences in their heads. They can also simulate the thinking of other people with whom they are in contact, a process that assists the leader in understanding and in being understood.
- **Critical thinking.** Recognitional decision making requires the leader to be objective in evaluating the likelihood that a particular action will achieve the desired outcome. He also needs to be alert to circumstances that might work against the preferred solution.
- **Adaptability.** Because many situations are fluid and information is uncertain, the leader needs to be willing and able to adapt "on the fly" as a situation unfolds.
- **Experience.** The "recognition" in this process depends on experience, and its different variants are essentially ways of drawing on experience. The wider the range of experience, the greater the likelihood that the leader can find an appropriate model. At a minimum, experience provides a context in which a decision maker can evaluate options. It may also provide "rules of thumb" that guide the decision process.[25]

---

[23] Klein uses "naturalistic" to encompass a range of different decision-making processes people tend to use when time pressures are severe or when information is ambiguous or missing (or both). His "recognitional" or "recognition-primed" decision making covers essentially the same range of decision models. "Intuitive" can be used similarly. "Heuristic," the adjective, is used to describe a decision process using trial and error rather than set rules (or, sometimes, a process involving "rules of thumb"), particularly when solving a problem for which no formula exists.

[24] This list is from the concluding chapter of Klein (1998), pp. 287–288. See also Cannon-Bowers and Salas (2000).

[25] More generally, we suggest that the key ingredient really is relevant *knowledge* of what kinds of solutions could work and what factors are most relevant. This knowledge can support recognition of analogous patterns and situations the leader has learned about through means other than experience, and our treatments here and in subsequent chapters will continue to recognize this. Practically speaking, experience weighs heavily—certainly in the contexts that Klein has studied, which include military decision making.

Many of these sources of decision-making power are not analytical. They do not absolutely require evaluation of all factors and alternatives; they allow accuracy to be traded away for speed when speed matters more.

To make this process work, the decision maker may implicitly consider various actions and assess their consequences from an objective standpoint. Or, as Klein observed in many cases of emergency operations, the decision maker may conceive of just one solution that "fits" and move immediately to implement it. But however it is done, a key feature of the process is the quick and implicit nature of the assessment and simulation, supported by a background of knowledge, experience, and intellectual abilities that take a long time to develop. Thus, this model applies directly to our description of situations faced in battle command: Klein's sources of decision-making power rely on experience, recognition, and understanding of context to get the leader to a good enough decision, soon enough to make a difference.[26]

The concept of "good enough, soon enough" is closely akin to a decision model called "satisficing" (combining "satisfying" and "sufficing") originally introduced several decades ago by Herbert Simon. Simon argues that "real human beings, of bounded rationality, cannot follow" a wholly rational theoretical optimization procedure. "Faced with complexity and uncertainty, lacking the wits to optimize, they must be content to satisfice—to find 'good enough' courses of action." This decision model is thus one of "bounded rationality," incorporating mechanisms for coping with complexities even when unable to resolve them. (Simon, 1979.)

In particular, and importantly for our purposes here, satisficing is a way around the fundamental problem that in the real world, complex situations do not readily yield up alternatives for action: instead, decision makers must search for them. And since the search space is theoretically infinite, the process needs a "stop rule"; military officers among others often term this the "good idea cutoff." The satisficing criterion illustrates such a stop rule: the search ends when a "good enough" alternative has been reached.[27] In the context of our work, we would posit that rather than any lack of what Simon calls "wits," it is the interaction of time constraints with complexity that generally drives operational decision makers to satisfice. Thus, Klein writes, noting that Simon was describing the behavior of business decision makers: "the strategy makes even more sense for fireground commanders because of their immense time pressure."[28] He makes the same case for military leaders.

---

[26] In contrast, "mechanistic" decision-making and problem-solving methods, while sometimes helpful, do not constitute a complete set of tools. By-rote application of the MDMP would fall into this category—which of course is why Army educators attempt to discourage such application.

[27] Simon (1979). His earlier works also discuss the concept, its theoretical underpinnings, and its applications at length. Cf., for example, Simon (1976).

[28] Klein (1998), p. 20.

It should be noted that satisficing is far more than simply a reflexive response, or a measured response in which one chooses the first feasible alternative. There is a significant amount of judgment and analysis involved in getting to "good enough," especially when there are high stakes and when alternatives that initially look good can have disastrous side effects. Even in the absence of the complexities of formal decision-making processes, leaders must be able to engage in some abbreviated amount of deliberation. And the keys to that process—and to abbreviating it—are critical thinking and a knowledge base that allows rapid evaluation of alternatives.[29]

This is not simply an academic viewpoint. In our discussions with Army leaders and educators concerned with leader development and battle command, we heard numerous variants of the conception formalized by Klein. Those directly concerned with decision making in military operations were particularly apt to articulate points such as these:

- Leaders must become more comfortable with ambiguity, better at fighting and making decisions under conditions of uncertainty.
- Too many junior leaders want to wait until every aspect of a situation and its possible courses of action have been analyzed.[30]
- We are too dependent on being able to predict all possible outcomes; we need to get leaders into a "comfort zone" where they are confident enough to make intuitive decisions (i.e., in our interpretation, comfortable with recognitional decision making).
- Intuitive decision-making ability is formed from experience; better intuition comes from better experience.
- You cannot really shortcut the amount of experience needed, but you may be able to concentrate and focus experience better.

The last two points bear some elaboration. The first is reminiscent of the old adage, "good judgment comes from experience, and experience comes from bad judgment." But the statement above is more applicable to our discussions here: The needed decision-making skills will grow out of "better" experiences ("better" in the sense of more sophisticated, more challenging, more evocative of a wide range of circumstances and challenges, etc.). The last statement implies a need for greater effi-

---

[29] It is more or less guaranteed, of course, that these short-cut processes will lead to a theoretically "suboptimal" decision: stopping the search when a good enough alternative is found is the essence of satisficing. Part of the process, then, must also be avoidance of alternatives that could have disastrous side effects. This can be a real challenge, particularly if a junior leader lacks full knowledge of the circumstances or intent of an operation. Since the aim is not to achieve a truly optimal solution but to take action that goes in the right direction and avoids catastrophic outcomes, a broad base of experience offers a defense against such outcomes.

[30] Once again, not a new problem. This is a criticism Rommel frequently made of his Allied opponents at far more senior levels.

ciency: Given the limitations on time to accrue experience and gain knowledge, leader development will need to pack more into existing tours or concentrate greater amounts of experience in fewer people. Both points are important in formulating leader development approaches, as we will argue in more detail in subsequent chapters.

Finally, some of our consultants pointed out that effective decision making is not the only outgrowth of possessing the skills we have been considering. Such skills also enable leaders to influence their circumstances, that is, to go beyond just adapting and reacting and take positive action in shaping those circumstances, on the battlefield or in other operational venues.

Summing Up: Decision Making in Today's Environment

These considerations lead us to a synthesis of the decision-making process that runs as follows. The essence of decision making is fitting available information together and choosing a course of action that matches both the problem and the opportunities that are available. In the military context this is essentially a process of problem recognition and solving, frequently in a compressed time frame and with high stakes. To effectively use recognitional decision making—to select the right context, draw on relevant experience and knowledge already gained, ask the right questions, achieve situational understanding, and apply it to make an appropriate decision—one needs especially:

- **Broad knowledge** of the many different factors that can bear on decisions in different command situations, to provide mental models against which new situations can be compared; and
- **General intellectual abilities**, such as adaptability and critical thinking, that facilitate rapid and well-informed decision making.

Of course, as our consultants emphasized, the knowledge and intellectual attributes must be grounded in a sound understanding of the principles of war and the tactical and operational fundamentals that grow out of them.

How do these traits combine to permit rapid and effective decision making? First, of course, the problem must be recognized, which is where previous knowledge and experience play such a crucial role. Then it requires understanding the opportunities that are (and are not) available and placing them in the context of circumstances, the desired outcome, and the capabilities and limitations of the resources at hand. The ability to place things in context is the core of what the Army refers to as "situational understanding" and its prerequisite, situational awareness: the ability to comprehend a situation in all relevant aspects of all attending circumstances.[31] In the process, the leader is expected to sift through all the information available (awareness) and construct an integrated picture (a "vision") of what is truly relevant and what it implies (understanding). Imagination, innovativeness, and critical thinking then permit the quick-enough development and selection of a course of action that will succeed.

Is this very different from the way that armies have always operated? We argue that it *is* different, because of the increased centrality of fast information processing and the consequent importance of situational understanding. Here, by contrast with other general traits and competencies emphasized in Army manuals, we find reason to believe there are notable departures from the past. To begin with, today's leader faces a wider and more disparate array of possible environments. Army units are often confronted with unfamiliar situations, enemies, and terrain. Many aspects of the operating environment are different from the traditional battlefield—for example, the presence of civilians who may be either friendly or hostile (or both). Consequently, information gathering is more difficult, there are more objects and conditions to track, and greater uncertainty surrounds them.[32] In spite of this complexity, decisions must be made under considerable time pressure, and often under the scrutiny of the media. Under these conditions, the simplicity and doctrinal neatness of MDMP may seem worlds away. Instead, the leader has to fall back on recognitional decision making, and he needs the skills and background that support it.

In addition, as many of our consultants have pointed out, the kind of warfare envisioned for future forces places a much heavier emphasis on the ability to capitalize on information superiority—the ability of U.S. forces to gather, sort, analyze, understand, and disseminate information better and faster than the opponent.[33] This "knowledge-based warfare" seems to many to be a fundamental paradigm shift. While we would argue that the shift is more like a trend, we agree that gaining full situational understanding is becoming more important, more complex, and more necessary at lower levels than before. More important, because doctrinal and opera-

---

[31] One could argue that awareness and understanding are nearly synonymous. In the Army's construct they are distinguished chiefly in that situational awareness is cognitive and situational understanding is conceptual. It is also useful to distinguish them in the contexts of training and education because they are taught in different ways.

[32] Some argue that because the U.S. military is striving to leverage technologies to produce more accurate and complete pictures of the operational situation, the resulting advances may reduce uncertainty and perhaps complexity as well. In many circumstances, as our consultants pointed out, technology can enhance situational awareness; and further technological advances are in the offing. However, the rest of the challenge is to get leaders sufficiently knowledgeable and adaptive to capitalize on the improved awareness. In addition, leaders must be able to develop understanding when the technology does not deliver, or when a situation is driven by factors that technology cannot cover.

[33] See, for example, U.S. Joint Staff, *Joint Vision 2020* (2000); and U.S. Army Training and Doctrine Command, *The United States Army Objective Force: Operational and Organizational Plan for Maneuver Unit of Action* (2002).

tional concepts are based in part on assumptions that U.S. forces will be able to capitalize on information dominance.[34] More complex, because there is a wider range of capabilities leaders must appreciate, more varied circumstances they must be able to comprehend, and a wider range of possible enemy responses in any given situation. More necessary at lower levels—implying decision making by leaders with less maturity and experience—because operational concepts and contemporary environments both work toward putting junior leaders into contact with a wider range of potential threats and circumstances.

So what does this imply about critical skills for future leaders? First, it must be said that many enduring attributes of leadership remain important. The time-honored attributes of character and general skills such as interpersonal and conceptual abilities will be as important as ever, essential for good leadership. Leaders who lack these traits will not succeed—regardless of their intellect and their operational and decision-making skills—because their subordinates will not follow them. Second, the general intellectual traits emphasized by recent perspectives—such as self-awareness, adaptability, and critical thinking—seem to warrant the increased emphasis that they are getting.

However, these general skills are not, by themselves, sufficient to support successful recognitional decision making. A third and indispensable ingredient is *experience*, the bedrock upon which a good decision is built. Both the Klein theory and the results of our interviews confirmed the crucial nature, indeed the centrality, of having a wide range of experience on which to base one's decisions. Experience, in a sense, provides the empirical support for applying a mental model, building a picture of the situation, and simulating the outcomes of various actions the leader might select. The wider the range of experience, the greater the likelihood that one will find a relevant past situation to use as a model. Thus, a world like today's, where the environments for future operations are unpredictable and highly variable, places a notable premium on having a stock of experience spanning many situations. In the next chapter we will describe our analyses of just how variable this environment can be and what that implies for specific skills that future leaders will need.

---

[34] This implies that it is crucial for leaders to be able to tell when they don't have that dominance. This was a topic of many a discussion, both in the field and in schools.

CHAPTER THREE

Key Leader Competencies for the Contemporary Operating Environment

Having examined the general make-up of the military leader persona and the knowledge and skill framework that it involves, we now examine some key operational skill requirements that we expect to change to a notable degree. We focus particularly on skills that contribute to capable battle command and decision making in both combat and noncombat situations.

Recent experience suggests that future U.S. military leaders will need to operate in more varied and complex environments than they have faced during the past 50 years. This chapter will argue that the root cause of this shift is the volatile nature of the missions, enemies, terrain, and battlefield conditions that characterize the new operating environments, as compared with the greater predictability and stability that prevailed during the earlier era. In addition, skill requirements may be affected by advances in technology and related changes contemplated in the Army's various plans for "transformation," which also are largely motivated by the changing environment.

We will describe how the evolution of the operating environment is likely to thrust leaders into unfamiliar situations and locales, under conditions where they need to seek new types of information yet make good decisions under considerable time pressure. Such changes, therefore, may pose serious challenges to a leader's ability to make a "good enough decision, soon enough." We see these challenges affecting leaders through three primary mechanisms:

- Increasing the *frequency* of operations in which leaders confront unfamiliar situations;
- Increasing the *complexity* of skills required;
- Involving *lower echelons* in more demanding roles, such as combined arms operations.

To explore these challenges, this chapter will consider three topics. First, we examine six key features of the contemporary operating environment that are likely to create challenges for future leaders. Second, we identify the nine most significant types of skills (or skill areas) that leaders will need to respond to those challenges. Third, we summarize our judgments by showing which skill demands are encountered most frequently, with increased complexity, and at lower echelons. Our analysis of these demands will then lead to discussion in the remaining chapters about the potential impacts on leader development programs.

Features of the Environment

Many observers have commented on the fluidity of the post–Cold War situation compared with the relative stability that preceded it.[1] In fact, the Army's doctrine community has worked for some time on cataloging aspects of the new context for military operations, dubbing it the "contemporary operating environment" (COE).[2] We adopt that terminology here, although a more accurate term might be environ*ments* (plural), given the multiplicity of different situations that U.S. forces may confront.

Despite this widespread perception that things have changed, we found no analytically oriented portrayal of *how* things have changed in ways that imply sharply different challenges for the leadership of units conducting military (either combat or noncombat) operations. Therefore, we undertook to identify the most important emerging challenges, based on a review of the military literature, particularly documents on the COE, combined with the real-world experience of Army officers who were recently assigned to RAND and had participated in one or more operations since 1990.[3] As our ideas about the environment developed, we also conducted a series of interviews with experts in military doctrine, officers serving in operational units, and academic personnel involved in teaching officers at Army schools.

As a result of that process, we identified six prominent but interdependent aspects of future environments that can be expected to influence the way the Army's units will conduct their operations. These form a foundation for identifying future leader requirements and challenges for leader development. As we will describe below, these key features are as follows:

- Wide variety of potential threats;
- Increased unconventional threats;
- Enhanced enemy capabilities in regional conflicts;
- Wide range of terrain types;
- Increased frequency of stability and support missions (rather than combat);

[1] There is indeed a very wide range of publications predicated on this observation. See, for example, Davis and Shapiro (2003), Cohen (2000), and Vinson (2000); for an earlier perspective, see Davis and Finch (1993).

[2] U.S. Army Training and Doctrine Command, *White Paper: Capturing the Operational Environment* (2000).

[3] These officers included a graduate school student and Army Fellows; their specialties included armor, intelligence, artillery, and medical support.

- Increased emphasis on information technology.

The first five aspects are drawn from our assessment of the COE, considering characteristics of future military operations (combat or noncombat) that directly affect leaders of tactical-level units. The sixth aspect is derived not directly from the COE, but rather from the Army's primary response, namely its plans for transformation toward a force structure and operational concept in which information technology and networking play a more important—some would even say central—role. Together, these six aspects of the environment encapsulate the far-reaching changes that are likely to challenge military leaders on the future battlefield.

Wide Variety of Potential Threats

The U.S. Army no longer faces a single, well-defined, predominant threat. In the future operating environment, the Army must be prepared to conduct operations against multiple threats with a wide range of capabilities.[4] The variety of enemies may be so large, and some so threatening in terms of their potential for thwarting U.S. goals and causing casualties, that the Army must focus a significant portion of training time and resources to address them. Threat capabilities will cover the spectrum from high-technology conventional warfare to low-technology unconventional tactics. Threats may arise from nation states or from non-state actors such as terrorists and criminals.

Recent operations illustrate this diversity. North Korea and Saddam Hussein's Iraq exemplify the traditional nation-state threat, presenting a potential for conventional mid-intensity or even high-intensity conflict. After Saddam Hussein's government was removed from power, that threat transitioned to an unconventional one. Units conducting operations in post-conflict Iraq were confronted with various enemy networks that included Saddam loyalists, radical Islamic fundamentalist terrorists from a variety of countries, organized crime, and disparate elements of tribal and ethnic groups attempting to manipulate U.S. forces and policy to their own advantage. Ten years earlier, Somalia presented an enemy of gangs run by warlords, competing for control of urban areas and scarce resources. In the mid-1990s, the operation in Bosnia aimed to separate ethnic populations intent on dislodging or destroying each other, both willing to inflict harm on U.S. forces if it worked to their advantage. Each of these kinds of threats must be handled differently and sometimes simultaneously.

---

[4] The Army of the Cold War had to be prepared to face different kinds of threats as well, but these were more peripheral and by and large did not occupy the main focus of Army doctrine and the readiness and training requirements that flowed from it. The difference now is that these more varied forms of threats are collectively the norm and not the exception.

Increased Unconventional Threats

Future enemies with limited resources relative to the United States are likely to concentrate their efforts against lucrative targets in "unconventional" ways. Compounding this is the adversary's willingness to engage in suicide attacks and to target noncombatants deliberately. Potential enemy activities range from the truly unconventional (nuclear weaponry, "dirty" conventional explosive packages, chemical and biological weapons) to unconventional uses of more traditional weapons (similar to past terrorist practices, but with new innovations). Even low-tech enemies may in some circumstances have access to some high-tech capabilities, such as the ability to disrupt information systems.

Disrupting the enemy's ability to engage in terrorist attacks will be a larger component of the overall challenge faced by leaders at all levels. Junior and mid-level leaders will thus be concerned not only with the traditional aspects of mission accomplishment but also with the need for force protection against a wider range of threats. Commanders will often need to allocate a larger portion of their capabilities and their attention to neutralizing enemy threats to friendly forces, to civilian targets, or to cultural targets.

Recent adversaries and operations in southwest Asia provide numerous examples of an unconventional threat. The success of coalition forces in the 2003 war in Iraq reinforces the generally held notion that the United States and its allies can quickly defeat enemy conventional forces, facing them with the choice of full capitulation or a move toward unconventional tactics. However, from the beginning of the conflict, enemy forces in Iraq conducted ambushes against forces on supply lines and in areas away from the main battles, along with suicide attacks and other forms of assault against checkpoints. Moreover, even after the end of large-scale conflict, terrorist activity continued against U.S. and allied targets in both Iraq and Afghanistan. Civilians who cooperate with U.S. forces have become targets. Enemy soldiers and other combatants dress in civilian clothes, drive civilian vehicles loaded with explosives, and hide weapons under civilian garments. The continued infliction of casualties is aimed at eroding support for the operation—particularly public support in the United States. These threats create new challenges throughout the depth of the battlefield, create confusion about where and who the enemy is, and clutter the battlefield with conditions that would not be expected when facing a more predictable, well-defined enemy.

Along similar lines, we note that North Korea is known to have chemical weapons and is pursuing nuclear weapons and their delivery systems. Additionally, North Korea possesses significant amounts of special operations forces and sniper brigades whose mission is to disrupt logistics and command and control.

Enhanced Enemy Capabilities in Regional Conflict

Although a peer competitor—an enemy that can match or nearly match U.S. capabilities across the operational spectrum—is unlikely in the near future, potential adversaries can certainly purchase commercially available technology that enhances their capabilities against friendly forces. They will pursue improved direct-fire systems, communication systems, missile technology, satellite capability, and countermeasures to advanced technology. Further, they will seek access to technology through both military arms sales and civilian technology markets; examples include a North Korean ship intercepted in the Mediterranean carrying SCUD missiles to a Middle Eastern nation, the French sale of Mirage jets to Iraq, and the Russian sale of GPS jammers to Iraq. High-resolution commercial satellite imagery is currently for sale via the Internet. High-tech communications systems are also readily available and adaptable for command and control. Finally, nations such as North Korea and Iran continue their pursuit of nuclear and other weapons of mass destruction (WMD). It is thus quite possible that future U.S. forces will either be attacked by nuclear or chemical weapons or be required to operate in a contaminated environment. They will certainly be called upon to operate in environments where they have to hedge against such threats.

Wide Range of Terrain Types

Historically, armies have gained leverage over adversaries by capitalizing on the natural advantages of different forms of restrictive terrain. However, until recently much of the focus of U.S. Army training has been on open terrain where the technological advantage of traditional heavy forces is maximized.[5] Future conflict seems much more likely to take place in restrictive terrain, as the enemy seeks to engage U.S. forces on land that negates their technological advantage. Thus, the Army may increasingly find itself fighting in urban, mountainous, and highly vegetated terrain.[6] Restrictive terrain provides advantages to the enemy by forcing the U.S. Army to employ its forces in smaller units, operating more independently and possibly with less coordination and control. It also provides natural shields to the enemy. Restrictive terrain complicates the operations of small units; it makes communication, reinforcement, sustainment, and mutual support more difficult. This is presumably less of a disadvantage to the enemy than to the United States—and thus a relative advantage to the enemy, particularly an enemy prepared to operate in and more familiar with restrictive terrain. Finally—and perhaps most important—the enemy will seek opportunities to fight in urban areas, where the added complexities of civilians on the

---

[5] Again we note that this is not an absolute distinction. Many Army units practiced for operations in restrictive terrain. But the primary focus, naturally enough, was on operations in the mostly open terrain that predominated in the primary threat scenario, mechanized warfare in Central Europe.

[6] U.S. Army Training and Doctrine Command, *The Operational Environment and Threat* (2003).

battlefield and the potential for damage to religious or cultural structures reinforce the challenges presented by restrictive terrain.

Recent history highlights the variety of terrain to which the Army could be exposed. The 2003 war in Iraq consisted of long movements over open terrain, engagements in outlying villages, and clearing operations in Baghdad—a city the size of Los Angeles. The fighting in Somalia occurred in the town of Mogadishu, a densely built-up area with narrow roads and congested neighborhoods. Korea consists of densely vegetated mountainous areas and complex, modern urban communities. The 2002 war in Afghanistan was fought in mountainous terrain at high elevations. Recent anti-guerilla operations in the Philippines were conducted in both urban and jungle environments. In sum, many signs point to the likelihood that military operations will be conducted in a variety of terrain types, and future leaders must be comfortable with them all.

Increased Stability and Peacekeeping Operations

If recent experience is any guide, the U.S. Army will be called upon to assist failed or defeated states in an attempt to effect a transition to democracy. Additionally, military force will be used to establish and enforce peace between warring factions to provide an opportunity for peaceful resolution of conflict. Recent operations in Haiti, Bosnia, Kosovo, Somalia, Iraq, Afghanistan, and Liberia exemplify the growing role of U.S. forces in stability and peacekeeping operations. Unlike traditional warfare, such operations require widespread interaction with civilian populations, coalition forces, civilian agencies, and nongovernmental organizations (NGOs). In such situations, the threat of ambush, civil unrest, and humanitarian disaster requires leaders to strike a balance between persuasion and use of force, often under scrutiny by the international press. At the same time, the threat of escalation to armed conflict requires the presence of trained combat soldiers and support personnel.

Leaders require a set of skills beyond combat proficiency to deal with the complex tasks of establishing or bolstering local governments, intelligence networks, and government services. In addition to their role as combat leaders, future leaders, even at the lower tactical levels, will need on occasion to act as civil servants, diplomats, mayors, city managers, negotiators, and police chiefs. They may need to easily transition from supervising a city council meeting to conducting raids on suspected enemy headquarters. The availability of a number of different possible sources of help in these kinds of tasks may make success more likely, but these same sources of support also increase the complexity of leadership.

Increased Use of Information Technology and Networks

A major force for change is the continuing advance of information technology and its incorporation into military organizations. Technological advances in communications, surveillance, and information processing will significantly alter the way forces conduct operations and promise to improve leaders' situational awareness.[7] For example, emerging Army doctrine envisions a different kind of unit that is designed to operate by capitalizing on technology that allows friendly forces to operate in different ways.[8] Under this concept, tactical networks will allow friendly forces to conduct military operations in restrictive terrain in dispersed formations. Initial study of digitized unit capabilities has led analysts to conclude that leaders and soldiers "will be removed in space more than ever before from each other, the systems they control, and the enemy they engage."[9] If such a concept matures into real-world units, the dispersion of forces, a result of technology and terrain, will require leaders at lower and lower levels to be facile with combined arms operations and capable of independent decision making to capitalize on short-lived opportunities.

Even more certain is an information explosion: digital networks and improved sensors will provide the leader with more data than ever before. The future challenge will frequently be not a lack of information, but rather a plethora of data requiring a leader to sort through multiple sources of battlefield information to arrive at a better informed, timely decision. Our discussions with Army leaders and trainers bear out that this challenge is real: modern information systems are helpful, but leaders can easily be inundated as they struggle to make use of the information to formulate orders. Perhaps now more than ever, leaders must become information managers, plucking out the critical pieces of information necessary for effective battle command and decision making.

Leader Skills

What leader skills are particularly important, considering these six aspects of contemporary and future operating environments? To address that question, we considered the circumstances of the future battlefield, looking for cues that point toward a set of leader skills necessary for success. For example, if the future battlefield will routinely present the leader with a variety of terrain types, then leaders can no longer be satisfied with the ability to envision a relatively open battlefield; they need to anticipate and *understand* the implications of all terrain types upon which a conflict may occur. Using similar logic and an operational perspective based on experience of the authors and our consultants, we identified nine important leader skills that seem

---

[7] We noted earlier the distinction between awareness and understanding. Technologies can increase the amount of information available and possibly improve its accuracy. The leader (and the staff) still has to make the leap to understanding. We deal primarily in this chapter with the ability to achieve situational *awareness*, noting that this is a necessary condition for the development of *understanding*.

[8] Department of the Army, Objective Force Task Force (2002). Numerous other sources advance similar views.

[9] Moses (2001), p. 29.

likely to present greater challenges in the future environment than they have in the past.

To provide an organizing framework, we outline these skills within the four major categories shown in Table 3.1. Each skill area refers to a broad understanding of key aspects of the battlefield and its environment. For example, category 1 refers to "understanding the enemy situation." In Army doctrine this is sometimes portrayed as a basic aspect of situational awareness, namely "seeing the enemy." However, our definition of the skill area goes beyond simply "seeing" or developing awareness of the enemy; it also encompasses an integrated understanding of the enemy's location, capabilities, and intent.

Similarly, the other categories refer to "understanding the physical environment" (such as terrain and structures in the area of operations); "understanding one's own capabilities and requirements" (such as knowing about and exploiting the Army's special strengths in combined arms operations and information technology); and "understanding social and cultural features of the environment" (such as the presence of civilians, coalition partners, and media in the area of operations).

All of these skill areas, of course, are closely related to situational understanding. Situational understanding is a necessary component of effective battle command and is built upon understanding all four of these items. Our focus, however, is not just on delineating those skills that underlie good tactical and operational leadership, but rather on identifying the degree to which emerging trends will pose more difficult challenges for leaders in the future.

Understanding the Enemy Situation

1. Understand the range and magnitude of enemy capabilities. While understanding the enemy has always been a critical dimension of battlefield success, the

Table 3.1
Categories and Skill Areas

Category of Understanding	Skill Area
Understanding the enemy situation	1. Enemy capabilities, location, intent
Understanding the physical environment	2. Urban terrain 3. Restrictive terrain
Understanding own capabilities and requirements	4. Joint and combined arms 5. Force protection 6. Application of information technology
Understanding social and cultural features of the environment	7. Civilian presence on the battlefield 8. Coalition partners 9. Media presence

increased complexity of the enemy has made this expertise more difficult to attain. Unlike the Soviet and Warsaw Pact threats that formed the paradigm for past assessments, the enemy of today and tomorrow can no longer be counted on to follow a reasonably well-established doctrine with easily identifiable weapon systems. The techniques of various enemy groups are more difficult to predict, the weapon systems are of greater variety (possibly including WMD), and various enemy groups have diverse religious, political, and even criminal motivations.

To understand such an enemy, leaders will need to analyze information from a wider variety of sources and assimilate that information into their operational vision. These sources range from high-technology sensor information to human intelligence gathered through routine interactions with the civilian population. Using this knowledge in concert with a best guess of enemy techniques and objectives, the leader will try to "get inside the enemy's head" and determine how he will fight. The increased complexity and amorphousness of the environment requires creative thinking and analysis to understand the enemy situation.

Understanding the Physical Environment

2. Operate in urban terrain. Urban operations seem likely to become the norm, rather than the exception. The increased likelihood of urban combat presents a set of challenges for the leader that need to be trained consistently across the force. Urban operations are no longer the sole domain—if they ever were—of light infantry units. Heavy mechanized units and other future units will need to operate in complex urban terrain while minimizing collateral damage. During urban operations the tactical array of forces may well differ from that on the more traditional battlefield. Accordingly, weapon systems must sometimes be applied differently, and command and control procedures must be adapted.

Fighting in urban environments is not new. However, it is difficult, tedious, dangerous work, and learning to do it well takes time away from training in other tasks—for example, large-scale rapid movement with concentrated firepower—whose expertise has also served American forces well in the past.[10] As a result, U.S. Army forces are not evenly trained in urban operations. The heavy force, in particular, has focused on combined arms operations in maneuverable terrain. The Joint Readiness Training Center has long included urban operations in its training scenarios, exposing light units to more frequent urban warfare. This expertise must be developed in heavy forces, since they are likely also to operate in urban environments, as they have been required to do, for example, in Iraq.[11] The National Training Center, the

[10] On the challenges of fighting in urban terrain, see Glenn (1998).

[11] Even though light forces have traditionally been the ones prepared for warfare in cities, Operation Iraqi Freedom saw urban operations conducted by the 3rd Infantry Division, 4th Infantry Division, 1st Armored Division, 2nd Light Cavalry Regiment, and 3rd Armored Cavalry Regiment.

Army's premier heavy maneuver training facility, is developing facilities for urban training. The leader development challenge is to develop expertise across the force, regardless of unit type. And both of these Combat Training Centers face the challenge of incorporating a host of diverse training needs—of which urban operations are only a part—into a limited amount of time for the units coming to train.

3. Understand the implications of restrictive terrain. The greater variety of terrain and the speed with which forces will be deployed to new areas of operation require a higher level of expertise in analyzing terrain from a tactical or operational perspective. Leaders at all levels will need the ability to quickly gain knowledge of the terrain and its implications for both friendly and enemy actions. That includes an understanding of how forces are affected by urban, mountain, or heavily vegetated terrain. The analysis process can be the same—consideration of factors like observation/fields of fire, cover and concealment, obstacles, key terrain, and avenues of approach (the traditional OCOKA)—but each terrain type presents different challenges. The increased challenge is twofold: understanding must be achieved faster, and it must be acquired in a variety of situations. Except for North Korea—and even this is debatable—leaders will be far less likely to have the luxury of "knowing the General Defense Plan like the back of their hands." Leaders frequently enjoyed this advantage in the past because they could examine and study the terrain first-hand, and they could rehearse on the ground they were going to defend. Friendly forces will not have the familiarity with the terrain they enjoy at home stations or training centers. The enemy is likely to have a much better appreciation of the landscape—an enhanced "home field advantage"—and U.S. Army leaders must be able to make up the difference under time pressure.

Understanding Own Capabilities and Requirements

4. Plan and conduct joint and combined arms operations. Apart from the features of the external environment, leaders are also facing an increase in the array of capabilities at their disposal. And because the challenges are so varied, leaders will have a greater need to understand the available capabilities and how best to capitalize on them. At the lowest levels, this requirement will manifest itself primarily as a broader understanding of the Army's combined arms capabilities. At higher levels—possibly as low as what is now battalion level—it will manifest itself as a broader understanding of both Army and joint force capabilities.

Combined arms operations will occur at lower levels for two reasons: restrictive terrain will compartmentalize units, and information technology and the greater mobility and longer ranges of weapon systems will combine to result in greater dispersion and decentralization. Junior leaders will need to understand better the capabilities of systems in all branches, not just their own, if they are to properly synchronize the forces at their disposal. Competence in combined arms will be increasingly important down to and including platoon level. This contrasts, by and large, with the more traditional single-branch focus of leaders in small units. Previously, platoons and companies have served as the training ground for gaining in-depth expertise in one's own branch, to be followed by exposure to other branches as the officer's career progressed. While this model is not wholly irrelevant in the new environment, the challenges of that environment make a broader understanding of total force capabilities more important at every level of command.

The trend in this direction has precedents in Army operations in Korea and is now showing up in contemporary operations elsewhere as well. Platoons in Korea frequently organize as combined arms platoons due to the restrictive nature of the defile fight. These formations consist of armor, mechanized infantry, light infantry, and engineers. This is sometimes a source of controversy, but it has proven advisable when the terrain does not permit a tactical array of more than a platoon's worth of vehicles. Similarly, the 3rd Armored Cavalry Regiment (ACR) often organizes a cavalry troop in a "quarter troop" configuration of 2 tanks and 3 scout vehicles under the control of a platoon leader, sometimes with other assets assigned to the platoon. Such task organization is becoming more frequent, increasing the demands for combined arms competence at the lieutenant (platoon leader) level.

Recent operations in Operation Iraqi Freedom caused the combined arms nature of stabilization operations to permeate down to very low echelons, as tailored forces were organized for conducting raids. Such raid teams typically consist of infantry, military police, counterintelligence teams, interpreters, and scouts. The leader also has an armor reaction force and aviation assets at his disposal. Air-ground integration to platoon level is critical for rapid response.[12] The Army has always emphasized combined arms operations, but the level at which they are being conducted is lower than in the past and occurs more frequently in the task-organized, modular configurations used for today's missions.

Army leaders will need a better understanding of the capabilities afforded them by the joint forces in which they will operate. Typically in the past, Army leaders at battalion level and below have had relatively little need to integrate joint force capabilities; this requirement was not prominent even at brigade level.[13] Contemporary and future operations, by contrast, are expected to require "continuous, simultaneous planning and execution *at all levels*."[14] This is in part an outgrowth of the greater ranges and lethality of modern weapon systems, the increase in range and coverage in communications and information systems, and of course the doctrine that capitalizes on these improvements. But we believe it is also an outgrowth of the changes in the

---

[12] Based on our discussions with leaders and trainers, reviews of after-action reports, and interviews with people who were directly involved in recent operations.

[13] This is not because the operations were not joint endeavors, but because the coordination and integration of the joint capabilities took place at higher levels.

[14] U.S. Joint Staff, *Joint Vision 2020* (2002). Emphasis added.

contemporary operating environment: the challenges faced by leaders at lower and lower levels are growing more complex and more diverse, so leaders will be better able to meet these challenges if they can comprehend and appreciate the possible contribution of the full range of joint force capabilities.

5. Protect the force against unnecessary casualties. Recent events illustrate the dictum that there will be no sanctuary in many future conflicts. Far more than in 20th century wars, rear areas[15] will be under constant threat of ambush, and forces of all types will require continuous and all-round security operations to protect themselves and their lines of communication.

Therefore, the leader will need to expand his awareness of force protection requirements. "Intelligence preparation of the battlefield" applies to the entire area of operations, not just those areas in which combat forces are seeking to engage the enemy, and will need to consider a variety of enemy perspectives. What might previously have been a routine logistics resupply route must now be analyzed in detail for likely ambush sites and potential enemy egress routes. Command post locations should be selected through careful analysis of enemy posture, and steps should be taken to protect command and control nodes from enemy attack. More forces may have to be committed to security operations, requiring creative means of managing forces to meet the mission requirements. All soldiers, regardless of their specialty, will need to be competent in security operations and actions on contact; combat discipline will be needed across units of every type. This force protection challenge increases the demands on the leader as the domain of threat analysis expands to include larger areas, more things that can be vulnerable, and a more complex enemy.

6. Apply information technology to improve situational understanding. Technological advancement in the Army requires leaders who are comfortable processing large amounts of information, communicating through a variety of media, and capitalizing on the advantages of technology. Leaders will need facility in using the technology to develop their own situational awareness and to communicate the resulting understanding to subordinates.

Recent research suggests that the training challenges for leaders are significant because they entail four levels of required competence: equipment operation, equipment application, systems operation and integration, and command and staff operations.[16] Leaders need to know more than the "knobology" of the new technology. They must understand the underlying technology's principles, know its capabilities, and know how to apply it in different situations to maximize the benefit. Once these

---

[15] The COE and current doctrine raise the question of whether this term is even relevant. Support forces and logistical and communications nodes will not seek direct combat, but the ability and proclivity of enemy forces to force them into direct combat has significant implications for commanders employing these forces.

[16] Moses (2001), p. 29.

skills are trained, the leader can begin to gain an advantage in situational understanding.

The ability to acquire large volumes of information brings with it the requirement that commanders and staffs be able to manage and sort information efficiently. If predictions of a faster pace prove justified, the increased speed of operations will require the leader to make decisions faster, even when operating in a dispersed fashion away from the next-higher headquarters. To make a good enough decision in a timely manner, the leader must process information at a speed commensurate with the pace implied by the environment.

Understanding Social and Cultural Features of the Environment

7. Conduct military operations with civilian presence on the battlefield. In all likelihood, battlefields of the future will have a variety of civilians present.[17] Managing refugees, interacting with urban populations, coordinating with NGOs, and controlling civil disturbances require skills different from traditional combat skills. Leaders will need to discriminate rapidly between hostile and nonhostile civilians during engagements. They will also need to be comfortable interacting with local agencies and political representatives in stability operations and, at times, to exhibit effective negotiation skills.

Missions in the Balkans, Somalia, and Iraq have shown the complexities associated with civilians on the battlefield. The dense population of Korea would certainly present refugee flow problems. Daily interaction with civilians is likely to become the norm in stabilization and peacekeeping operations. In such operations, soldiers and leaders need to easily transition from soldier to policeman and back again.[18]

The presence of civilians requires different communication skills from those developed in more traditional military contexts. This implies understanding civilians' objectives, methods, and responsibilities—essentially cultural and political understanding—and frequently as well the ability to communicate through a translator. Leaders need to become familiar with the key aspects of culture, politics, geography, and history that apply to the area where they are operating. Units may need to control civilian assemblies, or deal with groups "milling around outside the wire," which may or may not be innocent. Under other circumstances, leaders may need to rely on civilians as sources of intelligence and employ them to distribute information.

Similar considerations apply to dealing with local governments. Local governments may impose constraints, raise costs, or provide unique access to resources. Hostile or uncooperative local leadership, such as the various tribal chiefs in Somalia,

---

[17] This discussion refers to civilians not associated with the U.S. Army, such as local inhabitants and members of NGOs. Leaders also need to deal with Army civilians and contractors—whose presence is growing, especially in support functions—but managing them is beyond the scope of this report.

[18] Naylor (2003), p. 18.

presents a fluid picture of conflicting interests. Young leaders need to use caution in making commitments to local governments and to avoid promising what they may be unable to deliver.[19]

As urban operations and stabilization missions become more common, leaders will more frequently interact with civilians. These interactions require a different set of skills, at every level, that are not easily transferable from combat training.

8. Integrate coalition forces. Many future operations are likely to be conducted by coalitions, requiring leaders to integrate their operations, and sometimes their forces, with non-U.S. forces. They will need knowledge about the coalition partners' operating procedures, military customs, and military capabilities. Coalition forces have been involved in all recent operations. Peacekeeping operations in Bosnia included extensive partnerships with European partners. U.S. special forces units worked closely with the Northern Alliance during the war in Afghanistan. British forces assumed a key role in Operation Iraqi Freedom, and Iraq stabilization missions involve international forces.

Such coalition operations present a variety of challenges for Army leaders. As U.S. technology advances, integration with some coalition partners will be more difficult. Leaders will be required to synchronize non-networked and networked forces without violating operations security. Coordination through the use of an interpreter may be critical. As an example, consider operations in Korea, where platoon leaders are often required to coordinate with a Republic of Korea unit for a forward passage of lines or relief in place; typically, they can communicate only through an interpreter. This requirement affects all echelons, including lower tactical echelons, but is most intense for staff officers during the planning and execution phases of operations.

9. Interact with media. Broadcast and print media are likely to be present in almost all future operations. Embedded media brought live coverage of Operation Iraqi Freedom into households across the globe. Junior leaders and soldiers often found themselves interviewed in front of an international audience. That situation places a premium on knowing what to say, knowing how to interact positively with reporters, knowing how to cooperate with the media to ensure information provided from military sources is accurately reported, and understanding the potential impact of the presentation of an incident or story in local and international media.

---

[19] For an interesting perspective on many of these issues, see Lowe (2003). Numerous other stories support the same points.

Scenario Analysis

The above categories and skill areas are not intended to be an exhaustive, all-inclusive list of skills necessary for leader success in the contemporary and future operating environments. With the exception of the technological changes, none is entirely new. Rather, they represent competencies that may demand a broader background, more flexible approach, and greater degree of sophistication, possibly at lower echelons of command, than in the past.

So far, however, we have discussed these skills only as generalities with occasional illustrations. Before accepting them as truly critical competencies that leaders must master, one may raise questions that ideally would be answered based on experience or empirical observation. Were these skills actually important in recent operations, or will they be in operations for which the United States has planned? How frequently do they crop up in different scenarios, and are they common across many scenarios? Do they pose unusually complex challenges, compared with what units and leaders have encountered in the past? Do the skill requirements typically penetrate to the lowest echelons, such as companies and platoons, and, if so, is this different from previous experience?

To address such questions, we conducted an in-depth review of a number of operational scenarios that are rooted in real-world missions that the Army has executed or planned for in detail. Relying on our Army team members and project personnel with Army experience, we analyzed the following five scenarios, evaluating their operational environment characteristics and assessing the relevance of the leadership skills presented and their importance for success in each case:

- Korea
- Afghanistan
- Post-conflict Iraq
- Balkans
- Somalia

These scenarios range well across the spectrum of conflict. Korea and Afghanistan[20] represent mid-intensity conflict. Post-conflict Iraq may be viewed as a stabilization operation. The Balkan operations (Bosnia and Kosovo) represent peacekeeping operations separating warring factions, whereas Somalia represents humanitarian intervention in a failed state.[21]

---

[20] Both are at least mid-intensity. Korea offers the possibility of high-intensity conflict, i.e., operations in active nuclear, chemical, and biological environments. Arguably the other scenarios also carry this possibility, or at least the possibility of chemical and biological agents, as we note in our discussion here.

[21] Korea is a planning scenario, while the others represent recent or current real-world operations.

The material below reports our analysis of the five scenarios, organized by the four categories of leadership skills outlined earlier:

- Understanding the enemy situation;
- Understanding the physical environment;
- Understanding own capabilities and requirements;
- Understanding social and cultural features of the environment.

The discussion focuses on two major topics: First, how did these scenarios manifest requirements for the four categories of skills? Second, how important was it, in each scenario, for the leader to have competence in those skills?

Considering each skill area as a whole—for example, "ability to understand the enemy situation"—we judged how important it would be for the leader to possess well-honed skills in that area. This judgment depends on the skill's importance for mission accomplishment. Our judgments fell into one of three ratings:

- **Critical.** Competence in this skill area is essential for mission success. Without competence, the mission will fail, consume too much time, or impose an unacceptable cost in resources.
- **Important.** Highly valuable, but not essential for mission success. Lack of competence in this skill area will impede performance, but not necessarily to the point of mission failure.
- **Less important.** Competence in this skill area is helpful—it will help to make mission accomplishment easier, faster, perhaps more efficient—but it is not a key factor in accomplishing the mission per se; or competence is not required for the scenario.

It is worth reiterating that our judgments among these skill areas are *relative.* As stated before, we have determined that all of these skill areas require attention because their requirements have changed in some way as compared with past practice. The classifications above represent an attempt to differentiate the skills in this set *among themselves*.

Understanding the Enemy Situation

Our analysis of the enemy in the various scenarios, reported in Table 3.2, illustrates the need to take account of a wide spectrum of enemy capabilities, which we have arranged in three different categories: conventional, unconventional, and enhanced. On the high end, the North Korean army presents a capable conventional opponent who also possesses chemical weapons and uses unconventional tactics to disrupt the operations of supporting forces as well as combat forces. Certainly, among the ones

Table 3.2
Understanding the Enemy Situation

Skill Area Components	Scenario				
	Korea	**Afghanistan**	**Post-Conflict Iraq**	**Balkans**	**Somalia**
Conventional threat	NPRK army	Taliban army	None	Serbian army	None
Unconventional threat	Sniper, special forces, rear area threat	Terrorist attacks, disbanded Taliban, tribal factions	Terrorists, Saddam loyalists, tribal factions	Avoid major fights, small ambushes	Irregular forces, ill-defined and unstable ROE
Enhanced enemy capability	Chemical and/or nuclear weapons	Possible WMD	Possible WMD	None	None
Overall importance	Critical	Critical	Critical	Critical	Critical

we analyzed, the Korean scenario presents the greatest conventional warfare challenge. However, this is not the only scenario with a conventional threat. More common is the unconventional threat designed to avoid direct confrontation with conventional forces. Every scenario—notably including Korea—includes an unconventional threat, suggesting that future leaders will face this threat more frequently than planned for in the past. Finally, the possibility of WMD exists particularly in the Korea scenario so units must prepare for the possibility of operations in a contaminated environment, although such weapons have yet to be used against U.S. forces.

Our judgment was that for each of the scenarios we considered, leaders faced increased challenges in understanding the enemy situation, and meeting those challenges was critical. Of course, "understanding the enemy" has always been a prominent topic in treatises on military operations, and some degree of such understanding is required in any scenario. However, achieving this understanding is more difficult now than in the past. Korea is the only scenario with a well-defined, well-known enemy; even here, the enemy's ability to use unconventional forces and, for that matter, civilians would be likely to prove problematic. The other scenarios do not possess an easily identified or predictable enemy. There may be multiple enemy networks, each with its own objective and own tactics. There is less information for study, although current operations allow the building of an information base for future training. Even so, a characteristic of such enemies is that they do not follow a particular doctrine, and leaders must work very hard to predict new tactics that might be used by the enemy. For these reasons, understanding the enemy may be growing more difficult to achieve.

Understanding the Physical Environment

Table 3.3 describes analysis of the five scenarios as they relate to skill areas encompassing urban terrain and restrictive terrain. Without exception, each scenario provides significant terrain challenges. Korea presents challenges of every kind, from a variety of restrictive terrain to highly developed urban complexes. All other scenarios include many forms of restrictive terrain and varying degrees of urban complexity. This variety is a significant change from the past. Rather than fighting on open terrain that maximizes U.S. technological advantage, U.S. forces in such operations must cope with difficult terrain features in which unconventional forces seek to negate such advantages. Additionally, most scenarios have poor infrastructure, generally incapable of supporting heavy mechanized forces.[22]

With the exception of Afghanistan, where the heaviest fighting occurred in mountainous terrain, each scenario requires operations in urban terrain. Therefore, we rated skill at fighting on urban terrain as critical in all of the scenarios except Afghanistan. Likewise, restrictive terrain is a feature of four of the five scenarios. Post-conflict Iraq and Somalia present more urban operations and fewer involving restrictive terrain. For that reason we rated skill on restrictive terrain as only important in Iraq and less important in Somalia. Overall, however, it appears that the complexity of terrain will pose a significant challenge to leaders in scenarios such as these, particularly since so many Army units have traditionally trained on open terrain.

Table 3.3
Understanding the Physical Environment

	Features of Scenarios				
Skill Area	**Korea**	**Afghanistan**	**Post-Conflict Iraq**	**Balkans**	**Somalia**
Urban terrain	Complex urban terrain, many smaller towns	Small towns to medium cities, poor infra-structure	Complex urban terrain, many smaller towns	Small towns to medium cities, poor infrastructure for heavy forces	Smaller congested towns, poor infrastructure
Importance	Critical	Important	Critical	Critical	Critical
Restrictive terrain	Mountains, rivers, seasonal vegetation, rice paddies	Open desert, high elevation mountains, cave and tunnel complexes	Deserts, mountains, river valleys, swamps	Steep mountains, rolling plains, poor roads	Flat terrain and open spaces
Importance	Critical	Critical	Important	Critical	Less important

[22] We note that parts of the Army have always needed to prepare for the possibility of operating in restrictive terrain (and extreme climates). Today, however, such operations are more likely to be the norm, rather than the exception, in the spectrum of possible situations.

Understanding Own Capabilities and Requirements

Table 3.4 describes analysis of the five scenarios as they relate to skill areas encompassing friendly-force capabilities and requirements: joint and combined arms, force protection, and application of information technology. First is the ability to apply the capabilities of joint and combined arms forces. Our assessment concluded that in all scenarios, joint force and combined arms operations were at the core of the operation, regardless of the mission. Korea, of course, represents the most intense utilization of all battlefield operating systems (BOS),[23] including application of joint assets and capabilities. But all of the other scenarios also emphasized joint and combined arms operations, often at low echelons. In Afghanistan, for example, coordination between air and ground forces made a major contribution to swift victory. Even the less intense peacekeeping missions, such as the Bosnia operation, required routine combined arms activities.

One of the most prominent differences between the past and the future operating environments is the lower echelon at which combined arms and joint force operations may occur. In every scenario we examined, platoon-level leaders could be expected on occasion to integrate combined arms resources. More generally, combined arms synchronization is occurring at lower levels. While battalion is the traditional level of combined arms integration, these scenarios highlight cases where platoon-level combined arms operations are routine. Additionally, platoon leaders are more often operating independently, at least for short periods of time.

Furthermore, the continued introduction of advanced technology will place more emphasis on knowledge and skill in joint operations, beyond "combined arms" in the strictly Army sense. The importance of being able to appreciate and integrate a widening array of joint force capabilities compounds the complexity of the leader's challenge. Leaders will need this knowledge of joint operations possibly at levels as low as company (we occasionally heard platoon).[24] They will need this understanding at least to the extent of being able to form a complete vision of what is going on in their battle space (situational understanding), and this vision now more than ever should include joint force capabilities and methods.

---

[23] Battlefield operating systems are a convenient way of categorizing capabilities the commander employs (and integrates and synchronizes) to accomplish the mission and preserve the capacity to continue operations. There are seven BOS: maneuver; intelligence; fire support; air defense; mobility, countermobility, and survivability; combat service support; and command and control. Note that these are categories of capabilities, not units.

[24] One counterargument to this is that leaders, particularly at lower levels, need not be concerned with the source of a particular capability or how its effects are brought to bear—they need only concern themselves with the effects themselves. An example would be the use of fires delivered from a stand-off platform to destroy a target. The commander who needs the target destroyed, goes this argument, needs only to know how to request that the fires be brought on it; source and method would be transparent to the requester. Our discussions with a range of experts indicate that while this logic might hold true at platoon and possibly company level, leaders above those levels will more and more need a more complete appreciation of joint force capabilities and methods.

Table 3.4
Understanding Own Capabilities and Requirements

	Features of Scenarios				
Skill Area	**Korea**	**Afghanistan**	**Post-Conflict Iraq**	**Balkans**	**Somalia**
Application of joint and combined arms	High intensity joint and combined arms fight	Air-ground coordination, light infantry with organic BOS elements	Critical for raids: many BOS elements at platoon level	Primarily combined arms patrols with normal support, some civil affairs	Significant: special forces, rangers, infantry, aviation, Ethiopian armor
Importance	Critical	Critical	Critical	Important	Critical
Force protection	WMD, high-intensity combat, rear area ambushes, sniper, weather extremes	Terrorist attacks, extreme weather and elevation, difficult enemy identification	Terrorist attacks, extreme weather, difficult enemy identification	Unconventional attacks and ambushes, difficult enemy identification	Difficult enemy identification, unconventional tactics, ambushes
Importance	Critical	Critical	Critical	Critical	Critical
Application of IT for situational awareness	All dimensions of IT helpful	Helpful for terrain analysis and friendly situation; limited for enemy tracking and identification	Helpful for terrain analysis and friendly situation; limited for enemy tracking and identification	Helpful for terrain analysis and friendly situation; limited for enemy tracking and identification	Helpful for terrain analysis and friendly situation; limited for enemy tracking and identification
Importance	Critical	Important	Important	Important	Important

The second skill area listed in Table 3.4, force protection, is becoming increasingly complex and more central to all types of units. Force protection is complicated by the presence of civilians on the battlefield. Refugees and the local populace can be used as concealment for terrorists attacking U.S. forces. By integrating themselves with the civilian population, the enemy can make U.S. forces reluctant to return fire, increase the difficulty of enemy identification, and increase the likelihood of unacceptable collateral damage.

For these reasons, we rated force protection as critical in every scenario. The difficulty in identifying the enemy, the enemy's practice of attacking small, isolated units, and the media coverage given to casualties combine to highlight the importance of minimizing casualties. Additionally, the leader bears a professional responsibility to protect his force effectively. This task is assuming greater importance across all types of units; even the rear area is affected, as was illustrated by attacks on supply routes during the combat phase of Operation Iraqi Freedom. Thus, force protection involves not only the direct protection of one's own force, but the more complicated task of affording this protection more widely and without causing negative side effects.

In our view, the story is different for the third skill area, applying information technology to improve situational awareness. Typically this occurs through networked operations. Because of the characteristics of the enemy there, Korea is the only scenario for which network advantages are capable of assisting the leader in all three dimensions of situational awareness. North Korean main forces generally adhere to conventional norms by using conventional weapons and wearing military uniforms to identify themselves as combatants. These forces are susceptible to detection by the vast array of sensors designed to automatically detect the enemy and distribute accurate information through the tactical network. However, the advantage of sensors and networked information is less valuable in the other scenarios.[25] While information technology can help analyze terrain and blue-force tracking in any situation, it contributes less to forming an accurate picture of the enemy when that enemy uses less conventional forces and tactics, as we have recently seen in Iraq and Afghanistan. For example, detecting the enemy is more difficult when he wears civilian clothes to mingle with the population and conceal explosives. Sensors are unable to detect the difference between a pickup truck hauling produce to market and one transporting explosives to a checkpoint. Leaders must be able to use information technology for mid- and high-intensity conflict in scenarios such as Korea; but they also need to know how to track the enemy through other means, such as human intelligence from multiple sources. For that reason, we rated application of technology as important—not critical—in four of the five scenarios.[26]

Understanding Social and Cultural Features of the Environment

Table 3.5 summarizes how social and cultural features of the environment contribute to the challenges facing the Army's leaders. In every one of the scenarios, leaders were required to interact routinely with civilian local government leaders, the

---

[25] This also applies, of course, to those parts of the Korean scenario that involve North Korean unconventional warfare forces, which the United States would surely confront.

[26] This does *not* denigrate the overall importance of situational *understanding*; in fact, that understanding is critical. The issue here centers on the contribution of high technology to situational *awareness*, a precursor to understanding. In all of the scenarios except Korea, the benefits of technology in gaining situational awareness of the enemy are more limited, and other means, like human intelligence, are relatively more important.

We note that this point is controversial, and a counterargument may be made as follows. Current technology focuses on detecting and tracking fighting vehicles, aircraft, transportation and communication nodes, and the like—i.e., those features of military forces one would seek when facing a conventional enemy fielding armored and mechanized forces. It is possible that new technologies could detect unconventional forces by homing in on the kinds of things that lighter or unconventional forces carry—small arms, shaped charges, plastiques, and the like. Furthermore, it is entirely possible that technologies can further enhance the management, analysis, and display of human intelligence and other forms of intelligence. As such technologies are developed and fielded, leaders will need the ability to use them in virtually any scenario.

Table 3.5
Understanding Social and Cultural Features of the Environment

	Features of Scenarios				
Skill Area	**Korea**	**Afghanistan**	**Post-Conflict Iraq**	**Balkans**	**Somalia**
Civilian presence on the battle-field	Refugee flow, well-established local govern-ments	Daily contact with popula-tions, govern-ment officials, and NGOs	Daily contact with popula-tions, govern-ment officials; used as shields against U.S. forces	Daily contact with popula-tions, govern-ment officials, and NGOs	Civilians throughout urban areas; used as shields against U.S. forces
Importance	Critical	Critical	Critical	Critical	Critical
Coalition partners	Coordination required at all levels with ROK Army; potential for UN coalition forces	Special opera-tions integration with Northern Alliance; begin-ning NATO forces integra-tion	Multinational force drawn from diverse nations world-wide	Several Euro-pean coalition partners	Ethiopia, but limited inter-action with UN forces
Importance	Critical	Important	Critical	Critical	Important
Media presence	Possibly embed-ded media, but limited due to intensity of conflict	Media present throughout the area of opera-tions	Limited embed-ded media, but present in major urban areas	Media present throughout the area of opera-tions	Very little media presence during opera-tions
Importance	Important	Critical	Important	Important	Less Important

general population, or representatives of NGOs. Coalition partners and media partners are also present in each of the scenarios, although the degree of their presence varies with the political situation, intensity of the conflict, and nature of the mission.

Among these scenarios, one skill stands out: operating with civilians on the battlefield is a critical task across the board. In all scenarios, long-term (and arguably short-term) support for U.S. strategy is likely to depend on the Army's ability to conduct operations without causing major disruptions or casualties in the civilian populace. In many of the scenarios, in fact, a key objective has been to improve conditions for the indigenous population. Inflicting harm on civilians obviously runs counter to that objective, and undermines support among both the local population and the American public.

Integration with coalition forces is also rated critical in three scenarios. In Korea, platoon leaders must be able to coordinate with Republic of Korea forces for movement on the battlefield. In the Balkans, several European allies are a key part of the mission. In Iraq, the operation is formally a coalition activity, and a stated U.S. objective is to involve more international effort. Coalition integration seems likely to be an increasingly important aspect of future operations, so leaders down to platoon level need to know how to integrate with coalition partners.

Lastly, we rated interaction with the media as important but not critical in most scenarios. Primarily, this rating was given because of the variability of media presence at lower echelons. In some scenarios, media presence is prominent at the lowest levels throughout the battlefield. The emphasis of media coverage appears to be correlated with the political sensitivity of the mission, so it is not consistently present in all cases. This is not to deny that the international media may have long-term strategic implications; but relative to the other skills we have highlighted, skill at media operations appears less crucial to mission success.[27]

Summing Up: Challenges for Leader Development

We examined the above five scenarios in detail to provide a "real-world" test of the applicability of our concepts about the future environment and skills it may require. All of these scenarios either have already occurred or are the basis for defense planning; collectively they constitute a robust description of the contemporary and probable future environment facing military leaders. Since the skills we identified play an important role in almost all the scenarios, we conclude that they are prominent among the things that future leaders must master.[28] In that sense, all of them are important, and all deserve attention in the leader development system.

Beyond that, however, the above review suggests that the nine skill areas are likely to be *challenging*—perhaps too challenging—for leaders who are educated and trained under the system that has been in place up to now. This judgment of the challenge rests on the combination of three factors that indicate something has changed in a direction that may lead to a skill shortfall:

- **Frequency.** Numerous scenarios, spanning a range of conditions and threats, may call for the skill. In some cases the skill requirement is common across all scenarios. If a skill—such as operating on urban terrain—will often be needed but receives modest or uneven attention in the current system, future leaders are more likely to face challenges for which they are unprepared.

---

[27] Some observers have suggested that operating in a "media glare" requires greater media-handling skills on the part of the junior soldier. However, our interpretation is different, because we conclude that the requisite skills involve operational decision making but not media interaction. The platoon leader, for example, needs to make the right operational decision when confronted by a threatening group of civilians. Should he open fire on a hostile crowd, or tolerate his unit being pelted with rocks? How soon could he obtain help, and from where? The presence of media does not complicate this problem, but it certainly raises the stakes and thus places a premium on developing the right decision-making skills in junior leaders.

[28] The fact that future scenarios may not unfold as described here reinforces the need for leaders to be adaptive. They must also be confident enough in their training and education to be comfortable in selecting adaptive courses of action.

- **Complexity.** Future scenarios may present a more complex picture or situation than has previously been the case. An illustration is the ubiquitous presence of civilians on the battlefield; their presence profoundly affects tactics and calls for a deeper understanding and broader range of abilities than in traditional high-intensity warfare.
- **Lower echelons.** Future scenarios may require a skill in lower-echelon leaders, such as company commanders and platoon leaders, where in the past that skill (such as facility in combined arms operations) was typically well developed only in higher-echelon settings. The result could force development earlier in the career life cycle, affecting both school curricula and training regimens for lower-echelon leaders.

To sum up observations about the future challenge, we characterized these three aspects of the nine skill areas, as shown in Table 3.6. We also wanted to use this characterization to suggest a rough prioritization among the skill areas: Which skills are affected in all three ways, and hence may pose a particularly difficult challenge for the leader development system? We wish to make this priority distinction because constraints on officers' time and Army resources will surely limit how much effort can be invested in developing these skills. If tradeoffs must be made—even among these important skills—it is worthwhile to think through the priorities that might apply. Table 3.6 shows the results of characterizing the nine skill areas in terms of frequency, complexity, and lower echelons, and our resulting assessment of the degree to which they pose challenges for the leader development system.

Table 3.6
Factors Affecting Challenges for the Leader Development System

Skill Area	Frequency: Number of Scenarios Rated "Critical"	Increased Complexity	Challenges Increasing at Lower Echelons	Degree of Challenge
Force protection	5	X	X	Highest
Joint/combined arms	4	X	X	
Civilian presence	5	X	X	
Enemy situation	5	X		Medium
Urban terrain	4	X		
Restrictive terrain	3	X		
Application of IT	1	X	X	Lowest
Coalition forces	3		X	
Media presence	3		X	

NOTE: Entries marked "X" indicate a skill area that was rated as presenting increased complexity or challenges at lower echelons.

The skills are listed in three broad panels, roughly reflecting the extent of the challenge that we discern. The top panel includes skill areas that met all three criteria, while the middle includes skills that were rated critical in three or more scenarios and were also rated complex. The lowest panel includes skills that met the fewest criteria overall. Again we stress that the skill areas fall into this ranking *relative to one another*. For the reasons we have cited, all are important in an absolute sense.

Upper Panel

Skill areas in the upper panel were rated as critical in all or nearly all scenarios; they reflected a sharp increase in complexity facing the leader, compared with previous experience; and they presented demands on lower echelons unlike those in the past.[29]

For example, force protection has become critical in every scenario. It has also become more complex because it must be practiced in all parts of the battlefield and it must defend against numerous unseen threats—concerns that were much less salient in previous major conflicts. In addition, force protection makes greater demands on lower-echelon units of every type. Historically, all echelons have had some responsibility for security and force protection. However, on a linear battlefield, lower echelons were integrated into an overall force protection plan where the higher echelon provided a certain level of security. Additionally, the unit could position itself in an area where enemy contact was significantly less likely and force protection measures would thus be less demanding. This is no longer the case. Every echelon needs its own integrated force protection plan, and sanctuary is rare or nonexistent.

Similar comments apply to the application of joint and combined arms, and to civilian presence on the battlefield. Thus, the need for a comprehensive understanding of joint and combined arms capabilities is critical in almost every scenario. Employing these capabilities poses a complex challenge in coordinating disparate elements of the force and integrating them into a coherent whole—a task that used to be left to battalion commanders with fifteen to twenty years of experience, and to the commanders above them.[30] For example, in Korea restricted terrain requires platoons to task organize with tanks, mechanized infantry, light infantry, and engineers. Recent operations in Iraq had platoons organized with infantry, scouts, military police, intelligence specialists, and access to ready reaction teams and air support. Joint op-

---

[29] Implicit in all of these judgments is a comparison with previous experience—i.e., the leader development system under which the current generation of leaders matured. The benchmark for that comparison is the officer development model that prepared officers to fight the expected mid- to high-intensity conflict during the Cold War. During that time, the emphasis was leader preparation for intense combat against a relatively predictable enemy at predictable locations. The single future scenario provided a training focus that formed the basis for most tactical and operational aspects of leader development. In contrast, the current environment and our five scenarios that represent it vary in many ways from this implicit model.

[30] As we noted earlier, many would argue that battalion commanders would have been primarily concerned with combined *Army* arms, with joint force integration occurring occasionally at brigade level but more often at division level and above.

erations, or at least the ability to fully understand them as part of the operating context, are also extending to lower and lower levels. To prepare for these expanding challenges, the Army could need major changes in education and training; it may need to alter the single-branch orientation that typically characterizes positions and schooling for company-grade officers.

Civilian presence on the battlefield similarly fits into this high-priority group, but for different reasons. Not only are civilians ubiquitous in modern scenarios, their presence also complicates operations in many ways. With civilians in one's midst, it becomes more difficult to rely on firepower, and soldiers must work within restraints and rules of engagement that may more closely resemble police procedure than traditional military procedure. These restraints may also pose a threat of their own. Finally, the need to manage these problems affects all echelons. Whereas previous operations had higher echelons managing refugee flow and the primary requirement of lower echelons was to avoid civilian contact, lower echelons must now regularly interact with civilians. This applies even to an individual soldier or squad manning a checkpoint; surely a lieutenant needs to be ready for it.

Middle Panel

Skills listed in the second panel of Table 3.6 also pose challenges, but not in as many ways as those listed above. Skill at understanding the enemy situation, for example, is frequently needed and presents greater complexity than before, but it does not appear to require different or greater skills at lower echelons. Fighting on restrictive or urban terrain is also increasing in complexity; for example, it is more difficult to conduct operations in urban terrain while limiting collateral damage, and more challenging to fight in restrictive terrain in an information warfare environment. However, those skills are not always critical, and they also do not challenge lower echelons in unusual ways. For those reasons, we placed them in the middle panel.

Lower Panel

In the lower panel we list skills that, while still potentially challenging, meet fewer of the criteria and thus rank lower than the other skill areas in what—we stress once again—is already a highly selected group of skills.

Application of information technology was rated critical in only one scenario, even though when it does occur it increases complexity and affects lower echelons. Skill at dealing with coalition forces and media is sometimes critical, but often less so; and when present these requirements do not always impose a high degree of complexity. All of these skills, however, are increasingly needed at lower echelons. For example, in a networked environment, company commanders and platoon leaders have unprecedented access to information networks. Lower echelons are no longer dependent on FM voice communications, but have access to a much greater array of communications capabilities and displays. Coalition forces are integrated at lower levels in stabilization operations and in Korea. As previously stated, it is not unusual for a junior lieutenant to coordinate passage of lines or relief in place with a Korean unit. Lastly, embedded reporters expose lower echelons—platoon and even below—to daily interaction with the media. Public statements are no longer limited to the scheduled news conference, but occur at each echelon on the battlefield.

Implications

It is important to note that despite the nominal prioritization implied above, every leadership skill in this list is important, at least in some circumstances. Unfortunately, it would be difficult to change the leader development system to deal equally with all of them. The list includes many disparate skills, and many skills manifest themselves differently in certain scenarios. How, then, is the Army to deal with this variability, given the many other things that must also be done during an officer's career? Time—especially time to practice skills in units—is limited. This poses a genuine dilemma, because all the military services have traditionally relied on assignments in the operational environment to develop, hone, and deepen military skills. Indeed, a common view is that one can achieve a desired skill only through repeated experience in operational units—and preferably, not just serving in but *commanding* such units. Our review of the literature in Chapter Two showed a conceptual underpinning for this preference: It is through experience that one gains the background that permits "recognitional" or intuitively based decision making, especially when time is short and the stakes are high.

Thus, an officer traditionally spends time in tactical units as a lieutenant learning and practicing skills in leading a platoon and serving in staff positions at slightly higher echelons. Later, he spends time as a captain mastering company operations and gaining exposure to battalion and brigade staff work. Only later does he achieve battalion command, which builds on the same types of skills gained during previous tours. If the skills being learned follow a straightforward linear development process, that may work. In contrast, many of the skills we have studied above seem to depart from the traditional military or warfighting arena; they may pose genuinely new requirements in new domains that must be practiced in a special kind of unit or on a special kind of mission. In the next chapter we turn to this problem, seeking to understand the degree to which future leaders can be given enough time in operational units to gain experience in unfamiliar skills, while still meeting the traditional "gates" of career progression through successive grades.

CHAPTER FOUR

Experience Gained Through Operational Assignments

Analyzing Experience of Junior Officers

The foregoing analysis indicates that future Army leaders will face numerous challenges in operational decision making, due to changes in the operational environment, missions, force structure, and technology. These challenges will place a heightened premium on the leader's possessing well-honed operational skills and broad experience that covers a variety of missions and conditions. Leaders will need to be prepared to make quick decisions in unfamiliar circumstances and locales, under a pace of operations that everyone expects to be faster than in the past.

This chapter analyzes the extent to which future cohorts of Army leaders can actually gain this depth and breadth of operational experience, given the time they have during their careers and the many other things that officers must do. We focus here primarily on experience *in units*, which has always been the military's preferred venue for developing leaders and sharpening their operational skills. In selecting people for promotion and for command positions, the military system accords heavy weight to previous operational experience, and especially to previous successful *command experience*. For this analysis we accept that orientation, and we ask: How much experience can future leaders attain during their time in operational assignments? We also take into account the value of experiences in other organizational or institutional assignments—such as a Combat Training Center (CTC) observer-controller—that would develop an officer's understanding of operations and tactics.[1]

To gain quantitative insight into this problem, we developed a model of officers' assignments and other activities during the course of their early careers. The model was designed to explore the system's ability to impart more operational experience while still satisfying other demands (e.g., time attending professional schools or performing institutional functions). We focused on the sequence of assignments within an officer's career from lieutenant through major (i.e., grades O-2 through

[1] This is not to ignore knowledge and skills gained in other activities. Education and self-study, two other key methods of leader development, can play an important role, particularly in conveying the fundamentals. They can also be valuable in developing and refining critical reasoning skills. However, many officers believe that while education can impart basic knowledge, or "the what," there is no match for unit experience to practice "the how"—that is, the opportunity to personally experience leadership challenges and learn by doing.

O-4).[2] That segment of an officer's career covers the time from initial commissioning up to the point of promotion to lieutenant colonel and candidacy for battalion command. We reasoned that from battalion command through higher positions, the selection process is very stringent and the Army is likely to be able to find qualified candidates within the pool—provided that the pool of majors being promoted is itself well qualified. Thus, the object of the model is to assess how well the system can produce:

- Cohorts of officers who are well prepared to assume leadership positions within the grades of O-2 through O-4; and
- A cohort of officers promoted to O-5 who are well prepared for battalion command.

This analysis focuses on officers in the Armor branch, a subgroup of officers that is among those most heavily affected by recent changes in the operational environment and unit structures. Although other branches will experience similar effects, we judged that examining Armor officers would be a difficult "test case" and would reveal the intensity of any problems that recent trends may pose for the leader development system.

The next two sections of this chapter describe (1) the number and types of positions that officers must fill and (2) the way in which we represented officers' movements among those positions as they progress through the early and middle stages of their careers. The final section of this chapter then presents the results of analysis using the model.

Types of Positions

Four Categories of Positions

As a first step, we needed to identify the types of positions to be recognized in the analysis. There are, of course, thousands of distinct positions that officers can hold, but to consider the problem at that level of detail would make it intractable. We instead devised a set of categories that capture the essence of the challenge facing the Army, while omitting excessive detail.

We first distinguished positions according to the type of unit in which they are embedded: (1) operational units, known as TOE units; and (2) institutional units,

---

[2] All lieutenants, of course, begin serving at the grade of O-1 (second lieutenant) and soon progress to O-2 (first lieutenant). Personnel and training managers often combine those two grades and treat them as "lieutenants." We have done the same. Thus, in this report "O-2" means the aggregate of O-1 and O-2 positions.

Table 4.1
Four Types of Positions

Position Type	Abbre-viation	Definition	Examples
Leader	LDR	Leader in a TOE unit	Platoon leader (O-2), company commander (O-3), XO or S3 in a battalion or brigade (O-4)
TOE staff	TOE	Staff in TOE unit	Battalion or brigade S1, S4, Assistant S3, maintenance officer
Enhanced	ENH	TDA position that enhances operational/warfighting skills	Observer-controller at Combat Training Center, tactics instructor at Army school
Institutional	INST	TDA institutional position	Army or Joint Staff position, acquisition officer, doctrine writer

known as TDA.[3] TOE units are viewed as the primary training ground for tactical and operational expertise.[4] In addition, as we show in Table 4.1, we further subdivided both the TOE and TDA into two subgroups each. That created four major types of positions, replicated at each grade from O-2 through O-4. These position types differ in the ways in which they offer experience and the opportunity to sharpen tactical and operational skills.

TOE leader. First and foremost is a leadership position in a TOE unit. At the grade of O-2 (lieutenant), this is generally an assignment as platoon leader, the first command position that an officer holds. At O-3 (captain), the key leadership position is company commander. At O-4 (major), it is the job of executive officer (XO) or operations officer (S3) in a battalion or brigade. Strictly speaking, the XO and S3 positions are not "command" positions, but they are the most responsible positions held by majors, and those positions are widely thought of as essential "gates" on the way to further promotion in the Army's operational career fields. That is, virtually all future battalion commanders (and most lieutenant colonels) will be selected from those officers who have served as either an XO or S3.[5]

---

[3] Units classified as TOE (table of organization and equipment) are expected to deploy and conduct military operations. Units classified as TDA (table of distribution and allowances) do not typically deploy or engage in operations; they generally perform institutional functions such as training, acquisition, or headquarters staff coordination.

In addition, all officers spend some time as students in professional military schools. This school time, however, is not considered a unit assignment; instead, a holding account (TTHS—trainees, transients, holdees, and students) covers officers at school. Similarly, our model allots time for school attendance within an officer's career, but it does not explicitly represent school segments.

[4] In this chapter we generally use the term "operational" to describe the types of activities undertaken by units. We intend that this term be understood to encompass both "tactical" operations and more general military operations, including civil support and other noncombat operations.

[5] Each of the leadership positions named here is considered "branch qualifying" for the next grade (see Department of the Army, 1998). In practice, other leadership positions (including those within TDA units) are also

TOE staff. All other positions in a TOE unit, for our purposes, are treated as "TOE staff." Lieutenants, for example, may serve in junior positions in many types of TOE units (thereby gaining exposure to branches and functions other than their primary branch). Captains may serve on battle staffs at battalion or brigade level, or even division (thereby gaining appreciation for planning and operations of larger formations and combined arms).

TDA enhanced. This category constitutes a special subset of TDA positions that we judged were likely to sharpen and deepen an officer's operational skills. Included, for example, are observer-controllers at a CTC, where the job involves evaluating and critiquing the battle performance of units being trained. Similarly, we included some positions at schools—those that involve military science instruction of more junior officers—and some positions involved in tactical or operational training of Reserve Component units. We reasoned that immersing oneself in operational principles and techniques, in the role of observer-controller, instructor, or trainer, was sure to increase one's grasp of the associated skills. In addition, these positions—especially those at CTCs—are generally regarded as special jobs to which the most promising young officers are assigned, typically after they have become branch qualified. And the Army certainly has reason to regard such positions as important, given their role in training tactical units and developing future cohorts of leaders.

TDA institutional. The final category includes all other TDA positions, which encompass the majority of the TDA. These positions perform vital functions for the Army; they include the functions of recruiting and ROTC, initial training, professional education, weapons development, acquisition, financial management, coordination with other agencies of government, and a host of others. As a group, they perform the essential functions to maintain the Army, renew its stock of people and equipment, and develop and design its future course. However, we judged that serving in these positions, by and large, does not convey the same degree of operational expertise as the other three categories.

Battalion Commanders' Background

The prominence of the various types of positions can be judged, from one perspective, by examining the background of officers who are actually selected for senior operational positions. We developed our view of positions, in part, by analyzing data on the career histories of officers who had recently served as battalion commander in armor units (during 2001). Table 4.2 shows two illustrative cases from that analysis. Most of the commanders in our sample had similar histories.

---

treated as branch qualifying, even though they may not involve much operational experience. Given our focus on operational skills, we do not include TDA command positions within our leadership category. However, we will consider TDA leadership positions in certain special analyses later in this chapter.

Table 4.2
Assignment Background of Two Armor Battalion Commanders

Case 1: Armored cavalry squadron commander					
Asgt No.	**Months**	**Unit Type**	**Position**	**Location**	**TOE vs. TDA**
1	9	ACR	Tank platoon leader	Germany	TOE
2	10	ACR	Scout platoon leader	Germany	TOE
3	17	ACR	Cavalry troop XO	Germany	TOE
4	3	ACR	Assistant S3	CONUS	TOE
5	21	ACR	Squadron adjutant	CONUS, Saudi	TOE
6	20	ACR	Cavalry troop commander	CONUS	TOE
7	6	ACR	Cavalry squadron S3	CONUS	TOE
8	11	Test command	Test officer	CONUS	TDA
9	12	Armor/Mech Division	Tank battalion XO	CONUS	TOE
10	12	Armor/Mech Division	Brigade S3	CONUS, Balkans	TOE
11	17	Armor/Mech Division	Deputy division G3	CONUS	TOE
12	24	ACR	Cavalry squadron commander	CONUS	TOE
Case 2: Armor battalion commander					
Asgt No.	**Months**	**Unit Type**	**Position**	**Location**	**TOE vs. TDA**
1	4	Armor/Mech Division	Mortar platoon leader	CONUS	TOE
2	6	Armor/Mech Division	Tank platoon leader	CONUS	TOE
3	13	Armor/Mech Division	Company XO	CONUS	TOE
4	12	Armor/Mech Division	Battalion S4	CONUS	TOE
5	13	Armor/Mech Division	Tank company commander	Germany	TOE
6	16	Armor/Mech Division	Battalion HQ company commander	Germany	TOE
7	10	Armor/Mech Division	Assistant brigade S3	Germany	TOE
8	12	CTC	Computer operations officer	CONUS	TDA
9	12	CTC	Company team trainer	CONUS	TDA
10	24	School	Instructor	CONUS	TDA
11	10	CTC ACR	Regimental S1, OPFOR	CONUS	TOE
12	16	CTC ACR	Squadron S3, OPFOR	CONUS	TOE
13	11	CTC	Brigade S3 trainer	CONUS	TDA
14	25	Allied force	Exchange officer	Overseas	TOE
15	24	Armor/Mech Division	Battalion commander	CONUS	TOE

Case 1 illustrates the dominant pattern among officers who become battalion commanders of armor: Nearly all of their time is spent in the TOE Army. In the case of this officer, even the one assignment in the TDA was in a tactically relevant position—supervising tests of prospective new equipment within a test and evaluation command. Otherwise, this officer served in a sequence of TOE assignments, which are themselves instructive. As a lieutenant, this officer became a tank platoon leader, then commanded a scout platoon, and then was the executive officer of a cavalry troop. After some other TOE assignments, he became a cavalry troop commander. Later he was both a cavalry squadron S3 and tank battalion XO—key qualifying jobs for an Armor officer.[6] Then he served in brigade and division staff roles, including a deployment to the Balkans, before being promoted to lieutenant colonel and assuming command of a cavalry squadron. Notice also that his time was concentrated in armored cavalry regiments and heavy divisions, elements that are considered the premier training grounds for armor operations.

Case 2 represents a different battalion commander whose background includes more TDA time—but in very special TDA assignments. During his first 6 years this officer served only in heavy divisions, in the familiar sequence of key assignments (two platoon leader assignments, company XO, battalion staff, company commander, battalion and brigade staff). Then he served two assignments at a CTC, and later three more assignments—including a total of 61 months (or 5 years) at CTCs. That experience included both jobs as a trainer (for the "blue force" or training units) and as a leader of the opposing force (OPFOR) that confronts the training units. Moreover, one position in the OPFOR was as a squadron operations officer, a coveted and central position within the unit. Even his time as an exchange officer—in an allied nation—involved experience in that country's operating forces.

These two cases are typical of most officers in our sample of battalion commanders. They illustrate what kinds of positions are highly valued for their ability to impart operational skills, and illustrate why we focused on those types of positions in conducting our analysis of officer development. The common thread among them is the large proportion of time that such officers spent either in operational units or in other positions that deepen one's tactical and operational skills. Overall, in a sample of 23 battalion commanders we found the following modal pattern:

- 72 percent of assignment time at the grade of O-2 was spent as a platoon leader.
- 31 percent of time at O-3 was as company commander.
- 30 percent of time at O-4 was as XO or S3.
- Over the total career (O-2 through O-4), only 20 percent of time was spent in TDA institutional assignments.

---

[6] In the cavalry, a troop represents an echelon similar to a company, and a squadron an echelon similar to a battalion.

TOE Versus TDA: Army Requirements for Operational and Institutional Positions

Given the kinds of results we have just seen, it is no surprise that ambitious Army officers seek as many TOE positions as they can. However, as rational as this may be from an individual's perspective, it poses a problem for the Army. Although the Army desires to inculcate the maximum possible degree of operational experience in its officers, it needs officers to perform many TDA functions that contribute only marginally to developing tactical or operational skills. Figure 4.1 illustrates the distribution of officer TOE versus TDA positions in the Army as a whole.[7]

Figure 4.1
TOE Versus TDA Composition of Authorizations

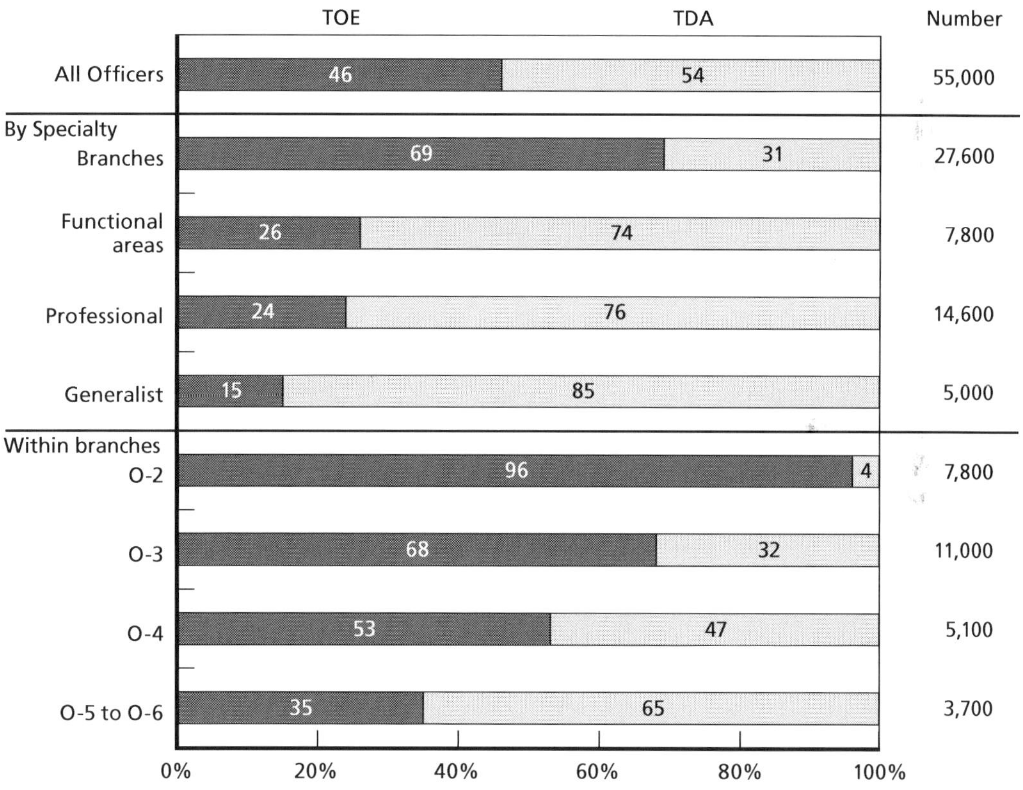

RAND *MG281-4.1*

---

[7] All of the analysis of officer positions is based on the September 2002 Personnel Manning and Authorization Document (PMAD), the Army's basic accounting tool describing the authorized positions that officers may fill. This document describes the Army's plan for the number of personnel, by grade and specialty, to be authorized in the future. Figures in this report cover only grades through O-6; they exclude authorizations for 380 general officers.

The top bar shows that the entire Army has authorizations for about 55,000 officers, of which fewer than half (46 percent) are in the TOE Army. Those 55,000 can be subdivided by specialty, as indicated in the second portion of the figure. A first distinction, important for our purposes, is between requirements for officers in "warfighting" branch specialties and others. The bar labeled "branches" represents 27,600 positions that call for a person from a specific branch.[8] As might be expected, the majority of positions calling for a particular branch specialty are in the TOE Army. However, even here it is notable that almost one-third of such positions are located in the TDA.

The next three bars represent other requirements for officers. These requirements are large, and they are concentrated in the TDA. For instance, about 7,800 positions call for a person from a specific functional area—not a branch. Another 14,600 positions call for an officer with a specific civilian professional identity, including medical personnel, legal specialists, and chaplains. These groups are managed very differently from branch specialists, and they do not "compete" for operational positions. Finally, some 5,000 positions are coded as requiring a "generalist." More than half of these are so-called branch immaterial positions, which can be filled by any officer; a minority of them require an officer from one of the combat branches.[9] Such generalist positions, particularly those unrelated to any particular branch, pose a further demand for qualified personnel because each branch—Armor, Infantry, Aviation, Signal, Quartermaster, and so forth—must supply its share of officers to fill those requirements.

Given these figures, one might expect that operational training opportunities are abundant in the warfighting branches, though limited in other specialties. However, this seeming abundance characterizes only the most junior grades. The bars in the lower portion of Figure 4.1, labeled "within branches," illustrate the variance across grades. For lieutenants (O-2), almost all positions are in the TOE Army; but TOE slots become increasingly scarce as one moves into the grade of captain (O-3) and higher. At O-3, TOE slots account for about two-thirds of the total, and at O-4 about half. At O-5 and O-6, only about one-third of the positions are in the TOE. Thus, as officers are promoted through their careers, they encounter relatively fewer positions that offer operational experience and relatively more positions in the TDA.[10]

---

[8] Included are all recognized branches, whether they are designated combat, combat support, or combat service support. Those three groups did not differ substantially with respect to their TOE-TDA proportions. Collectively these branches comprise the bulk of the Army's Operations Career Field.

[9] Combat branches, in this definition, include armor, infantry, field artillery, aviation, air defense artillery, special forces, and engineers.

[10] They also encounter the need to be assigned to generalist positions, whose numbers climb from 2 percent of O-2s to nearly 20 percent of O-6s.

This distribution is important because it limits the number of positions that "produce" operational experience and defines a large group of positions that "consume" it. Although the TDA positions (with some exceptions as noted earlier) may not be regarded as producers of operational skill, they are certainly consumers, in the sense that TDA officers by and large need some operational background (and currency) to perform well. No one would be comfortable, for example, if the officers manning weapons development, acquisition, or central planning staffs were deficient in operational knowledge. Even functions that may seem far removed from the operational world—such as recruiting—are often manned by seasoned soldiers who have an exemplary background in operations. Indeed, to the degree that any function requires a uniformed military officer, there are arguments why the incumbent should possess appreciable experience in the basic operational function of the military.

This poses a basic issue of breadth versus depth. Possessing many non-operational jobs, the Army faces a choice of having (a) a smaller number of people with extensive time in operational units or (b) a larger number of people with, on average, more modest exposure to such units. Moreover, the emergence of "new" demands—such as the more varied demands of the contemporary operating environment or evolving technology and organization in transformed units—intensifies this tradeoff. New environments (such as peacekeeping in the Balkans or stabilization in Iraq) are likely to require different skills or a different experience base—preferably previous experience in those "new" missions and environments. Greater operational skill may be needed for positions in units that are "new" in structure or operational concept, such as Stryker brigades. All of the trends we reviewed in Chapter Three point in this direction. Thus, the Army faces a situation in which it may need increased time to develop officers in more varied operational skills, and yet it must continue to "pay the bill" for officers who must man the TDA, with its important but non-operational functions.

This is truly a conundrum because the various needs of the Army work in different directions: some considerations argue for operational expertise, while others argue for other skills. In almost all of the above, and in the analysis we will shortly present, we have concentrated on the importance of operational qualifications. The Army's inclination, we believe, will lean similarly toward maximizing leaders' proficiency in that general area. However, although operational skills are often viewed as paramount, there are at least three cogent counterarguments in favor of "breadth":

- Operational leaders must know the TDA; they must understand what the Army's institutions are capable of delivering and how they fit into the larger picture. Likewise, officers in TDA institutions need understanding of military operations and currency in associated concepts—otherwise they are likely to guide their institutions in directions that do not match the Army's operational needs.

- Senior leaders will emerge predominantly from operational specialties. As they rise in grade, the demands on them will broaden; they will confront broader problems at echelons above division and in positions that involve contact with other national institutions (such as Congress and state and federal agencies) and international institutions (such as alliances, coalitions, and the United Nations). These senior officers need knowledge of institutions across and beyond the Army.
- The future may hold different operational demands, or it may make them less relevant. It would be unwise to invest all of the officer corps' professional time in the specifics of current tactics, techniques, and procedures. A robust system will develop officers who have become comfortable with adapting their knowledge and skills to unusual challenges and can thus better meet the demands of an uncertain future.

All of these arguments merit consideration in the analysis. While operational expertise is desirable, it comes at some cost in narrowness. That tension motivates the key question that our analysis will address: How much operational experience can the Army provide future leaders, while still filling all the demands upon it and preserving some breadth?

Modeling Officer Careers Through Key Positions

Number of Positions for Armor Officers

We now describe how the model represents key positions and patterns by which Armor officers move through those positions along career development paths. Table 4.3 exhibits the number of positions that need to be filled by Armor officers, by type of position and grade. These estimates were based on the Army's official authorization database for 2002, modified slightly to reflect the categories we discussed previously.[11]

This table reconfirms a point mentioned earlier. TOE leader positions dominate the total for O-2s; at the higher grades, however, there are fewer TOE and more TDA requirements. Operational training opportunity—defined as TOE leadership, TOE staff, or TDA enhanced—is relatively abundant among lieutenants; of the 903 slots calling for an Armor officer, 93 percent are operational. The picture is different

[11] We made some interpretations to enumerate TOE leader and staff positions, and to identify TDA positions regarded as "enhanced." Those categories are not directly represented in the PMAD database, our source for authorization data. Also, we added a small number of positions to account for "generalist" requirements (also called branch immaterial and combat arms immaterial positions). See the appendix for our interpretations and method.

Table 4.3
Total Positions to Be Filled by Armor Officers, by Position Type and Grade

Position Type	O-2	O-3	O-4
TOE leader	760	226	94
TOE staff	77	279	29
Enhanced TDA	0	117	53
Institutional TDA	66	307	156
Total	903	929	332
Percent operational[a]	93	67	53

NOTE: The total includes both Armor branch officers and Armor's "fair share" of generalist positions.

[a]"Operational" is defined as including TOE leader, TOE staff, or enhanced TDA.

for captains and majors, however. Among captains, 67 percent of all slots are operational, and among majors 53 percent are operational.

The Development Paradigm: Career Segments

The model was designed to represent sequences of assignments—called *paths*—that involve the above positions. In our model we made several simplifying assumptions about the number of assignments and their relationships. Our ultimate objective was to explore the effects of changing preferences for operational experience—particularly for "new" positions. Thus, we deliberately chose to simplify other features of the personnel system, such as perturbations in tour lengths and numbers of assignments, to construct a model that would reveal the most important changes.[12] Table 4.4 shows the basic structure that we used.

In this representation, a career consists of three grades, each of which begins with a period of professional education ("school") and contains two or three unit assignments ("segments") thereafter. The time periods shown are nominal, but they were designed to represent reasonable amounts of time consistent with the promotion points and assignment patterns found in today's force. As will be seen, our model also allows departure from these basic patterns to explore the implications of others.

---

[12] Of course we recognize that this representation omits many details. In real life, there may be millions of paths. An actual operating system would need to move individuals on different schedules and allow for unanticipated events (such as resignations, illness, or decisions to change branch). Nevertheless, we argue that our representation captures the essentials of experience patterns, and because certain elements have been abstracted, it allows us to focus on the details of sequences rather than other phenomena that are less central to our problem.

Table 4.4
Development Paradigm: Segments within Grades

Grade	Event	Assignment	Months	Cumulative Months	Cumulative Years
O-2	Lieutenant school	—	6	6	0.5
	Assignment 1	1	18	24	2.0
	Assignment 2	2	18	42	3.5
	Attrition	—		42	3.5
O-3	Captain school	—	12	54	4.5
	Assignment 3	3	24	78	6.5
	Assignment 4	4	24	102	8.5
	Assignment 5	5	24	126	10.5
	Attrition	—		126	10.5
O-4	Major school	—	12	138	11.5
	Assignment 6	6	18	156	13.0
	Assignment 7	7	18	174	14.5
	Assignment 8	8	18	192	16.0
	Attrition	—		192	16.0

For example, in this system an officer begins his career with the basic leader course—here assumed to last 6 months, which allows for other courses, such as Ranger and Airborne—and then has two unit assignments as a lieutenant, each lasting 18 months. That brings him to the promotion point at 3.5 years of service. At that point, the cohort of lieutenants undergoes attrition (because some leave the Army or transfer into another branch or career field), and the remaining officers are promoted to O-3 in the Armor branch.

At O-3, new captains are assumed to spend their first year completing their previous assignment and attending the captain's course at school. Most captains remain in that grade up to about 10 or 11 years of service, so this system has room for three O-3 assignments of 24 months each. At the end of that period, namely 10.5 years of service, the captain cohort again undergoes some attrition, with the remainder being promoted to major.[13] At the grade of O-4, a similar pattern applies, except that there is less time for each assignment (18 months per assignment) before the cohort reaches the promotion point to O-5 (16 years).

Three particular features of this representation should be borne in mind. First, the model actually represents only unit assignments. School attendance is assumed for everyone newly promoted to a grade, but it is not modeled explicitly. That atten-

[13] See the appendix for information about implied flow patterns and sources of attrition. These patterns result in a system whose promotion points and retention patterns are similar to the Army's observed patterns in recent years.

dance is represented here as the first event after promotion, but actually it could happen anywhere within the grade.[14] Second, each assignment has a fixed length within a grade. Thus, every assignment for O-2s and O-4s lasts 18 months, and every assignment for O-3s lasts 24 months. Third, attrition is "bunched" together at a point between grades, rather than being spread continuously throughout the grade. Although these simplifications depart somewhat from the reality of personnel management in today's Army, we believe that they are reasonable ways of describing a future Army for the purpose of examining the accumulation of operational experience.

Sequences of Assignments

The above structure implies several different patterns, or sequences of assignments, that could be included in an officer's career at each grade. The varying patterns occur because at each segment, one may be assigned to any one of the four position types (subject to certain rules that we will explain in a moment).

Patterns for lieutenants. Table 4.5 shows the simplest set of possibilities, those that apply to lieutenants.

In this system, every lieutenant begins his career as a platoon leader (PL). Normally, this assignment is in one's basic branch; for Armor officers, that would mean leading a tank or cavalry platoon. Then the officer may go into one of three other assignments, creating the three patterns listed in the table. In pattern 1, the officer receives another assignment in a leadership position: either to lead a second platoon (typically in another branch or function, such as support), or to serve as a company executive officer, the number two position in a company. Officers who receive that assignment pattern are regarded as having two "leadership" experiences as lieutenants, a pattern that promotes operational expertise.

Table 4.5
Sequences of Possible Assignments: Lieutenants (O-2)

Pattern	Assignment 1	Assignment 2
1	PL	PL*
2	PL	TOE
3	PL	INST

*Can be either a second PL or company XO assignment.

[14] To represent such varying patterns would produce a considerably more complex system with many more paths. Even our simplified system requires some 51,000 possible paths, which makes the problem large but still tractable for optimization. We imposed these restrictive assumptions specifically to keep the problem manageable, while preserving the ability to examine the phenomena in which we are most interested. Our experience suggests, however, that those assumptions could be relaxed in further analysis, if it seemed necessary to increase fidelity.

In pattern 2, the officer goes to a second assignment as a TOE staff member, but not as a leader. That pattern also conveys operational experience, but not as much operational *leader* experience as pattern 1. In pattern 3, by contrast, the officer goes to an assignment in the institutional TDA. That pattern would be regarded as less desirable from an operational development point of view, since the last 18 months of his lieutenancy are not likely to deepen his proficiency in operational matters.

Patterns for captains. The picture becomes considerably more complicated at higher grades because there are more segments available and there are some additional rules that the Army would be likely to impose. As we specified the system, there are two key rules. First, no captain will serve as a company commander immediately upon promotion. Instead, the first assignment will be of a nonleadership type, to season the captain before he takes on a leadership role.[15] Second, no captain can be assigned to a TDA enhanced position until he has served as a company commander. That is, he must accrue the critical experience of command at the O-3 level before the Army will entrust him with the demanding duties of an enhanced position.[16] These two rules result in the 20 patterns shown in Table 4.6.

The upshot of these rules is that every captain begins his tenure in either a TOE staff position or a TDA institutional position. Some officers then move into company command (CDR), while others stay in TOE staff jobs or move into an institutional job. Some who do not get command at assignment 2 do get it at assignment 3, although there is the possibility (as today) that a captain will never get a TOE company commander job. There is also the possibility that some will receive two TOE company command jobs; this is difficult to achieve in today's Army, but it does occur and would naturally convey a deeper amount of operational experience. Finally, there are two paths that result in assignment to an enhanced TDA position during assignment 3, after the officer has served as a company commander.

Patterns for majors. At the grade of O-4, the assignments change but the patterns are formally equivalent. That is, the patterns shown in Table 4.6 apply to majors in the same way, except that the position of CDR (company commander) is replaced by the position of XO/S3 (which we use here to mean either an XO or S3 job). Again we specified two rules: no major could become an XO or S3 during his

---

[15] We recognize this does not always happen. Senior commanders whom we have consulted on this and other projects have almost always cited this as a desirable goal, so we model it this way.

[16] This is essentially how the Army operates today. That is, most captains begin their tenure in a staff position or TDA assignment, and only later do they assume company command. To be deemed qualified for a CTC or key school teaching assignment, the Army would want them to have company command under their belt; in fact, the strong preference would be for an officer who led a TOE company, although previous leadership in a TDA company may be accepted if circumstances require it.

Table 4.6
Sequences of Possible Assignments: Captains (O-3)

Pattern	Assignment 1	Assignment 2	Assignment 3
1	TOE	TOE	TOE
2	TOE	TOE	INST
3	TOE	TOE	CDR
4	TOE	INST	TOE
5	TOE	INST	INST
6	TOE	INST	CDR
7	TOE	CDR	TOE
8	TOE	CDR	INST
9	TOE	CDR	CDR
10	TOE	CDR	ENH
11	INST	TOE	TOE
12	INST	TOE	INST
13	INST	TOE	CDR
14	INST	INST	TOE
15	INST	INST	INST
16	INST	INST	CDR
17	INST	CDR	TOE
18	INST	CDR	INST
19	INST	CDR	CDR
20	INST	CDR	ENH

first assignment as a major;[17] and no major could be assigned to an enhanced TDA position until he had completed an XO or S3 assignment. The result is that all majors, like captains, begin with service on TOE staff or in the institutional TDA, and then move into leadership and enhanced positions as opportunities and time permit. Since the categories and rules are parallel to those for captains, in the case of majors there are also 20 possible patterns. That does not mean, however, that the actual flows of personnel will be equivalent. The flows will be influenced by the distribution of positions within the grades and by other considerations to be described below.

Rules Governing Selection for Positions

The above categories establish a framework of positions and general rules by which officers can be developed, but they are not complete. They allow a vast number of possible *solutions*, that is, feasible combinations of paths such that all positions are filled at all times and no officers are "left over" without a position. The purpose of

---

[17] Again we note that this is not always possible but commanders do desire it.

the model is to explore possible solutions, so that we can say, for example, that in order to fill the positions given the rules, we would need X number of officers following path A, Y number following path B, and so forth.

Given the large number of possible solutions, we need some criteria to choose those that are acceptable; we know that the Army would not be indifferent to all paths or all solutions. The personnel system (and the model) would need a set of preferences to choose among paths, placing certain officers in positions for which their background makes them preferred. For example, the Army would prefer company commanders and XOs to have extensive operational backgrounds.

We simulated this selection process by establishing a schedule of *point scores* that favor certain types of background when selecting candidates for a particular position. We then programmed the model to make assignments such that the total of points accrued, across the entire force, was maximized.[18] For example, to fill an XO position at O-4, we would prefer—other things equal—an officer who had:

- At last one TOE company command;
- Multiple platoon leader assignments;
- More rather than fewer assignments in TOE units at O-2 and O-3;
- Enhanced TDA experience at O-2 or O-3;
- At least one TOE assignment at O-4;
- A previous tour as an XO or S3.[19]

The schedule of point scores encourages assigning people with the most intense operational preparation to leadership positions; it allots fewer points when filling other positions. For example, a person with a preferred operational background would generate a high number of points when filling an XO position; but a person with the same background would yield fewer points when filling a TOE staff job and still fewer when filling a TDA institutional job. In this way the model proceeded to select feasible solutions that would fill all positions with all officers at any given time, but with the goal of maximizing the system's total point score.

---

[18] Each path in the model carried a profile recording the officer's background on a number of characteristics relevant to selection for future positions (number of O-2 leadership jobs, number of company commands, number of TOE assignments, enhanced experience, etc.). At each segment, the model evaluated these profiles by looking up the points we had allotted for persons with that profile when being considered for the particular position to be filled. See the appendix for the schedule of points awarded to different profiles for each type of position.

[19] In later replications of the analysis, we distinguish service in "new" units from "old" units. In those analyses, the scoring schedule recognized additional preferences for new-unit background when filling positions in new units (see the appendix for details).

Analysis Results

Base Case: Emphasis on Operational Background

Table 4.7 shows the set of paths that the model selected to meet the above rules for assignment while also ensuring that all positions are filled.[20] In this table, each row represents a *path*: a unique sequence of unit assignments that an officer can follow over his career. Each column represents a particular segment of an officer's career: two segments at grade O-2, three at O-3, and three at O-4. Each cell entry indicates the position that the officer fills on that path at that segment.The Personnel Manning Authorization Document (PMAD) structure that we replicated in the model calls for 301 officers to enter each year to sustain the system.[21] However, the system does not require 301 separate paths. Many officers share a common path, such as the 79 entrants who follow path 1. Altogether, the model was able to fill all positions and maximize point scores using just 9 paths, as shown in the table.

Each entry is coded with an abbreviation and shading to indicate leadership and other operationally relevant features of the position, as shown in Table 4.8.

Table 4.7
Assignment Sequences: Base Case Maximizing Operational Background

Path	No. of Entrants	O-2		O-3			O-4		
1	79	PL	PL	TOE	CDR	ENH	TOE	XO/S3	ENH
2	27	PL	PL	TOE	CDR	ENH	INST	XO/S3	ENH
3	40	PL	PL	TOE	CDR	INST	INST	XO/S3	INST
4	30	PL	PL	TOE	CDR	INST	INST	XO/S3	ENH
5	22	PL	PL	INST	CDR	INST	INST	XO/S3	XO/S3
6	8	PL	PL	INST	CDR	ENH	INST	XO/S3	ENH
7	14	PL	INST	TOE	CDR	INST	INST	XO/S3	XO/S3
8	51	PL	TOE	TOE	INST	INST	INST	INST	INST
9	30	PL	INST	TOE	INST	INST	INST	INST	INST

Key: PL = platoon leader; TOE = TOE staff; CDR = company commander; ENH = enhanced TDA; XO/S3 = brigade/battalion XO or S3; INST = institutional TDA.

---

[20] Procedurally, these paths were selected by an optimization algorithm that maximized total point scores (derived from assignment rules) subject to constraints that filled all positions. See the appendix for the point schedule and optimization method.

[21] However, not all 301 persons remain at each stage. To sustain the PMAD-driven structure, the Armor branch must lose some fraction of the original entrants at each grade. Some of these people leave the Army, but many enter other branches, functional areas, and so forth. See the appendix for attrition rates that were imposed to meet the constraints of the PMAD structure.

Table 4.8
Coding of Positions in Path Displays

Position code	Position Description	Color Coding
Leadership Positions in TOE Units		
PL	Platoon leader (O-2)	Dark gray
CDR	Company commander (O-3)	Dark gray
XO/S3	Battalion/brigade XO or S3 (O-4)	Dark gray
Nonleadership Positions		
TOE	TOE staff (i.e., any TOE position other than PL, CDR, or XO/S3)	Light gray
ENH	Operational skill-enhancing position in a TDA organization	Black
INST	Institutional position in a TDA organization	White

To illustrate, consider path number 1, which incorporates the greatest degree of operational experience among all the paths in the table. A total of 79 officers will enter the Army each year and follow this path. The sequence of assignments along their path is represented as follows.

- **Assignments at O-2.** Each officer receives two back-to-back assignments as a platoon leader during his service as a lieutenant.[22] Because they are leadership jobs, they are displayed in dark gray.
- **Assignments at O-3.** When the officer is promoted to captain, his first assignment is in a TOE position (typically on a battle staff), but not as a company commander. That assignment is displayed in light gray to convey the idea that the position tends to enhance operational skills, but not to the same degree as command. In his second assignment, the officer becomes a company commander (now shown in dark gray because it is a leadership position). Thereafter, in his third assignment, the officer fills a TDA enhanced position (shown in black), which further develops his operational skills.
- **Assignments at O-4.** Upon promotion to major, the officer's first assignment is to a TOE job (light gray). Then he receives a leadership assignment, either as an XO or S3 (dark gray). Following that, for his third assignment at O-4 he receives another TDA enhanced assignment (black) appropriate for a major.

Path number 1, of course, represents a career that is very rich in tactical and operational experience. It contains four assignments to leadership positions and two

[22] Procedurally, these paths were selected by an optimization algorithm that maximized total point scores (derived from assignment rules) subject to constraints that filled all positions. See the appendix for the point schedule and optimization method.

other TOE assignments. The other two assignments are to TDA positions that enhance operational skills, such as being an observer-controller at a CTC or a military science instructor at an Army school. Most of the other paths contain a substantial number of leadership and TOE assignments, but not as many; instead, officers on those paths spend some time in institutional jobs and many have no enhanced assignments. The limiting case of this group is path number 9, which is followed by 30 entrants. Those officers receive only one leadership assignment, as a platoon leader, plus one TOE assignment. The remainder of their career is spent in institutional positions.

On average, this system produces a cohort of officers at O-4 who have a considerable degree of operational experience, as indicated by the preponderance of leadership, TOE, and enhanced assignments appearing in most of the paths. That is a consequence of the rules that we set up to establish preferences for operational background among officers entering key assignments. For example, when filling a company commander position, this system prefers officers who had two platoon leader jobs rather than one; if such an officer is not available, then it prefers someone who had one platoon leader job and a TOE assignment over someone who had a platoon leader job and an institutional job. Similarly, in filling a TOE XO or S3 position, the system prefers officers who had greater amounts of experience, rather than less, in company commander, platoon leader, TOE, and enhanced positions.

The overall result of the system in Table 4.7 is concentration of TOE experience in O-4 leaders and officers who fill enhanced positions such as observer-controller and school instructor. To convey an appreciation for the depth of the operational preparation afforded to this cohort of officers, below we assess it along three key dimensions.

Preparation of XO/S3s in TOE units. Consider first the background of officers who enter a position as battalion/brigade XO or S3. The officer development system should ensure that officers entering these influential positions have considerable operational experience. In Table 4.7, those positions are located within paths 1 through 7, which together cover 220 entrants. To assess their preparation, note first that all of them were commanders of TOE companies before they became XO/S3s. Second, most of them also had a TOE assignment during their captaincy (paths 1–4 and 7). Among the remainder, those on path 6 had a tour in an enhanced position, and those on path 5 received double (back-to-back) XO/S3 assignments. Third, the XO/S3s spent most of their preceding Army careers in operationally relevant positions: in either TOE leadership or TOE staff or enhanced positions.[23]

---

[23] Various metrics can be used to show this. A simple calculation is as follows: Note that the XO/S3 assignment typically occurs at segment 7 of a career; thus there are 6 preceding segments that can provide preparation. Across the 7 paths that involve an XO/S3 assignment, there are in all 42 preceding segments (6 × 7) among the paths that lead to XO/S3. Among those 42 segments, 69 percent (a total of 29 segments) are "operational" (TOE leader, TOE staff, or enhanced).

Preparation for O-5 leadership. Another way of assessing the leader development system is to consider the background of the cohort of O-4s who have served as XO/S3s by the time they can be promoted to O-5. To assess their operational qualifications, we could consider the history of all 8 segments in such officers' careers up through the end of their service at O-4. Here again the cohort shown in Table 4.7 has considerable credentials. First, note that by the end of their time as O-4s, 73 percent (220 of 301 entrants) had the experience of commanding a TOE company *and* serving as XO/S3 in a TOE unit. Second, about two-thirds of that group (144 entrants) also had the benefit of an enhanced assignment; in fact, about half (114 entrants) had *two* enhanced assignments, one as a captain and another as a major.

Preparation for enhanced positions. A third way of assessing the system is to examine its ability to place highly qualified officers in the enhanced positions, where they will be teaching and critiquing the performance of units and other officers. On this dimension too, the system in Table 4.7 appears effective. For example, every person entering an enhanced position has already served in the leadership position (company commander or XO/S3) appropriate for his grade. Paths 1 and 2, which supply the lion's share of enhanced positions, have particularly intense preparation; their assignment sequences consist almost entirely of TOE experience and previous enhanced experience. Finally, nearly 80 percent of the officers who enter enhanced positions at O-4 (paths represented by 114 of 144 entrants) previously held an enhanced position at O-3.

Thus, the system represented in Table 4.7 provides a high degree of preparation for future TOE leaders. That should not be too surprising, since the scoring schedule governing assignments was designed to encourage that kind of preparation, to the maximum extent possible. Still, the configuration of required positions could have prevented such a high degree of preparation—for example, if there had been many more non-operational positions that needed to be filled.

In fact, the configuration of positions does have one notable effect on the feasible set of outcomes: namely, it limits the number of officers who can receive intense operational preparation. In this solution, that phenomenon appears in the last two paths (8 and 9). Officers who follow those paths receive little operational experience at O-3 and none at O-4. Instead, they serve one TOE assignment at O-3 (segment 3) and then remain in institutional TDA positions for the remainder of their career. This occurs because the PMAD contains many TDA institutional positions that officers must fill.[24] Since the preference rules that we established route many officers into repetitive TOE assignments—such as those in paths 1 and 2—it becomes necessary for other officers to follow repetitive TDA assignments in order to fill all the requirements. This illustrates the inherent tradeoff between maximizing operational

[24] At grade O-3, TDA institutional positions account for 33 percent of all positions. At O-4, they account for 46 percent.

experience for leaders and extending a modicum of operational experience to all officers.[25]

A Comparison Case: The "Legacy" System

To gain an appreciation for how much experience is being accumulated and how it might compare with historical norms, we compared the above base case with a "legacy" system. In simulating that system, we attempted to set preferences geared to the rules by which the officer management system has historically operated. In this case we implemented rules that tend to value command—either in a TOE or TDA unit—as a way of producing the maximum number of officers who may be deemed "branch qualified."[26] That is, under the legacy system the scoring schedule accorded the same point score for a previous TOE command as for a previous TDA command; both were treated as branch qualifying. The model's optimal solution for that system is shown in Table 4.9. This table displays the same position coding as before, except that here we distinguish two command positions, shown in bold: (1) commander of a TDA company and (2) XO/S3 in a TDA organization.[27] Other than making this distinction, the personnel structure for this case is the same as in the base case.

Several features of this solution are notable. First, it is possible to accomplish the basic goal of providing every officer a command opportunity during his tenure at O-3 and O-4. Notice that in Table 4.9 every captain serves as a company commander, either in a TOE or TDA unit, and every major serves as an XO or S3. Therefore, they all become branch qualified, under the official rules for managing the officer personnel system.

However, achieving that goal comes with some drawbacks from the standpoint of accumulating operational experience among officers who are heading for leadership positions. For example, some majors, at the time they assume an O-4 leadership position, have less TOE command background. Paths 5, 7, and 9 exhibit this feature; officers on those paths eventually become XO or S3 in a TOE unit, but they have

---

[25] It is possible, in principle, to avoid keeping officers in successive TDA institutional assignments by imposing preferences for retaining officers who are on paths leading to future leadership qualification. We experimented with mechanisms that would allow higher retention rates for paths 1–7 and lower retention rates for paths 8–9, and the model was able to fill all positions by not retaining people on institutional-intensive paths after the grade of O-3. All of those on the paths that continued to O-4 had company command assignments, and most had XO/S3 assignments at O-4. However, the Army cannot control retention to that degree, since the decision to remain in the Army or in the branch is partly determined by the officer. Therefore we continued with the specification we had adopted at the outset, which imposes a uniform retention rate across all paths.

[26] See Department of the Army, *Commissioned Officer Development and Management*, DA Pamphlet 600-3 (1998).

[27] These are the only TDA command positions at grades O-3 and O-4. There are no leadership positions in TDA organizations at O-2.

Table 4.9
Assignment Sequences: Legacy Case

Path	No. of Entrants	O-2		O-3			O-4		
1	64	PL	PL	TOE	CDR	ENH	INST	XO/S3	XO/S3
2	50	PL	PL	TOE	CDR	ENH	INST	XO/S3	ENH
3	9	PL	INST	TOE	CDR	CDR	TOE	XO/S3	XO/S3
4	1	PL	PL	INST	CDR	INST	INST	XO/S3	ENH
5	6	PL	PL	TOE	**Cdr-TDA**	INST	TOE	XO/S3	ENH
6	31	PL	PL	TOE	**Cdr-TDA**	INST	INST	**XO/S3-TDA**	INST
7	25	PL	PL	TOE	**Cdr-TDA**	**Cdr-TDA**	INST	**XO/S3-TDA**	XO/S3
8	1	PL	PL	INST	CDR	CDR	TOE	**XO/S3-TDA**	XO/S3
9	28	PL	PL	INST	**Cdr-TDA**	**Cdr-TDA**	TOE	**XO/S3-TDA**	XO/S3
10	51	PL	TOE	TOE	CDR	INST	INST	**XO/S3-TDA**	ENH
11	35	PL	INST	TOE	CDR	INST	TOE	**XO/S3-TDA**	ENH

never commanded a TOE company. Overall, only 68 percent of the entrants on paths containing a TOE O-4 leadership assignment (XO/S3) would have prior TOE company command experience.

A related problem applies to officers who move into enhanced positions at O-4. In paths 10 and 11, officers entering an O-4 enhanced job had a TOE company command but never held an XO/S3 position in a TOE unit. And in path 5, people entering an O-4 enhanced job had an XO/S3 position but not a TOE company command. Altogether, 64 percent of people on paths that culminate in an O-4 enhanced position are affected by one of these two limitations. Because enhanced positions involve teaching, evaluating, and critiquing others on operational performance, this lack of background would be viewed as a drawback in the system.

On the other hand, the system in Table 4.9 has one distinctive feature that many would value. In this system, few officers are limited by a path that keeps them in TDA institutional assignments for most of their career. For example, paths 6 through 11 have a considerable amount of time in TDA institutional positions. However, persons on all of those paths except path 6 eventually return to the TOE Army. This pattern may be compared with the patterns in Table 4.7, where many officers get repeated assignments to TDA institutional positions. In fact, 27 percent of the Table 4.7 cohort (paths 8 and 9) receive little operational experience after their lieutenancy, and none of them gets company command in a TOE unit. The reason for this is that other officers—those in paths 1 through 6—are racking up assignment after assignment in TOE units and enhanced TDA jobs. Thus, the system of Table

4.7 provides more concentrated operational experience to a subset of officers, but at the cost of diverting another subset from repeated TOE and leadership experience.

A related consequence of the base case in Table 4.7 is that quite a few officers serve in senior TDA institutional positions without having recent TOE experience. Consider, for example, a major in the last segment of path 9. His last exposure to the TOE Army would have been as a junior captain—some five assignments before (about seven years earlier). Is this a problem? That depends on the threshold and recency of TOE experience that one would like to have in TDA position incumbents. That same officer would have had 24 months of early TOE experience (including a battalion or brigade staff job) plus 18 months as a platoon leader. Some might view this as less than desirable preparation for TDA service, particularly as a major.

Overall, the above analysis illustrates two key points. First, it is definitely feasible, given the Army's officer personnel structure, to provide future leaders with more concentrated, sequential experience in operational leadership and staff positions. Second, this comes at a price: when some officers receive more intensive and in-depth exposure to operational experiences, others will get less, and the difference is quite noticeable. Our base case achieves a remarkable degree of operational background in its O-4 leaders, but it also requires an appreciable fraction of officers to forgo repeated operational assignments and opportunities to command tactical units. Thus, there is a tension between giving future leaders operational depth and giving all officers broad experience. While we do not wish to prejudge the overall value of those two opposing goals, we did want to explore how far the Army could increase leader operational experience if it chose to do so. Therefore, in our further analysis, we assumed that the paramount goal for the future would be to achieve the greatest possible operational depth in leaders; thus, we adopted the preference scheme corresponding to Table 4.7.

Developing Experience in "New" Units

The solutions we have just described apply to an Army in which all units are of uniform type. However, one of our principal questions is: What happens when the Army creates "new" units, such as units that undertake very different types of missions, or units whose transformation produces a very different set of capabilities and experience demands? If such changes increase the demand for expertise in new units, can the Army implement developmental sequences that will build the necessary depth in their officers?

To examine that possibility, we elaborated the model to recognize two different types of units, which for shorthand purposes we call "new" and "old." We then populated the model with a modest number of new units and instituted different preferences when filling positions in new units. For example, when filling new-unit leadership positions, we might prefer officers who have a greater degree of overall operational experience or officers who have previous experience in a new unit—or both.

We stress that the designation of "new" is not meant to apply only to a particular plan for transforming units or to any particular kind of unit. A new unit could be one that is performing a different mission, such as unconventional warfare in Afghanistan, peacekeeping in the Balkans, or occupation duties in Iraq, even if its structure remains the same. The key attribute of a new unit is that *its leaders will need to draw on some different skills and aptitudes, and thus may require a different, and more demanding, preparation process.*

Recognizing the difference between assignment to a "new" unit and an "old" unit creates a large number of additional position types. For example, each leadership position (PL, CDR, and XO/S3) and each TOE position may occur in either an old or a new unit.[28] However, recognizing just the leadership and TOE distinctions expands the mathematical problem notably; applying the rules we stipulated above, our formulation yields a total of 51,030 possible paths.[29]

For a first look at the effect of this distinction on assignments, we designated a modest-sized subset of units as "new."[30] We also made a small adjustment in the preference scores for assignments; when filling a position in a new unit, the scoring scheme awarded a small additional amount to prospective candidates who already had served in a new unit before. We then ran the model with those parameters, which produced the paths shown in Table 4.10.

This table reflects a new notational convention to distinguish new versus old unit assignments. Assignments to old units are shown in heavy black type; assignments to new units are shown in heavy white type. For example, path 1 begins with two assignments as platoon leader in a new unit (in heavy white type). Path 1 then continues with one assignment to a TOE position in a new unit (also in heavy white type). For the next assignment, however, the officer is assigned as a company commander in an old unit (heavy black type). Later the same officer receives two TDA institutional assignments, followed by two assignments as XO/S3 in an old unit.

Although that particular path is mixed, the preferences driving the model endeavored to permit officers to receive repetitive assignments to new units. Paths 2–7 reflect the degree to which such repetitive patterns proved feasible. In path 2, for example, the officer begins with two assignments as platoon leader in new units; later the Army is able to capitalize on his early experience in new units, because he serves

---

[28] We did not distinguish new versus old assignments to enhanced or institutional TDA positions because we judged it unlikely that the Army would establish entirely different CTCs or schools to deal with the new set of missions or the new set of transformed units.

[29] See the appendix for the procedure that generated those paths.

[30] As a starting point, we designated all positions in units that had significant numbers of Armor officers and that were currently being reconfigured, or might soon be reconfigured, as of 2002 (see the appendix). Those units included about 12 percent of all leadership positions as "new." In a later excursion, we will investigate the effect of increasing the number of new positions.

Table 4.10
Assignment Sequences: New and Old Units

Path	No. of Entrants	O-2		O-3			O-4		
1	16	PL	PL	TOE	CDR	INST	INST	XO/S3	XO/S3
2	8	PL	PL	TOE	CDR	CDR	INST	XO/S3	XO/S3
3	4	PL	PL	TOE	CDR	ENH	INST	XO/S3	XO/S3
4	5	PL	PL	TOE	CDR	CDR	INST	XO/S3	XO/S3
5	3	PL	PL	TOE	CDR	ENH	INST	XO/S3	XO/S3
6	5	PL	PL	TOE	CDR	ENH	INST	XO/S3	XO/S3
7	1	PL	TOE	TOE	CDR	INST	INST	XO/S3	XO/S3
8	14	PL	PL	TOE	CDR	INST	INST	XO/S3	INST
9	42	PL	PL	TOE	CDR	INST	INST	XO/S3	ENH
10	79	PL	PL	TOE	CDR	ENH	TOE	XO/S3	ENH
11	7	PL	PL	INST	CDR	INST	INST	XO/S3	XO/S3
12	23	PL	PL	INST	CDR	ENH	INST	XO/S3	ENH
13	1	PL	TOE	TOE	CDR	INST	INST	XO/S3	XO/S3
14	50	PL	TOE	TOE	INST	INST	INST	INST	INST
15	44	PL	INST	TOE	INST	INST	INST	INST	INST

NOTE: Within the gray shading, heavy black letters indicate positions in "old" units; heavy white letters indicate "new" units.

two tours as company commander and one tour as XO/S3 in new units. There are limitations on such repetitive assignments, primarily arising from the small number of new unit positions available. However, by scanning down the paths in Table 4.10 one can observe that all paths that begin with a new-unit assignment also contain later segments in new units. Perhaps more importantly, every company commander or XO/S3 serving in a new unit has already served in a new unit; typically, he has had more than one such assignment. So, this pattern builds up new-unit experience and produces a cadre of officers with some depth in the special requirements of the new environment.

How well are leaders prepared under this scheme? In the new-unit paths (primarily numbers 1–6), every company commander receives three or more back-to-back assignments in TOE jobs (that is, two platoon leader jobs and one TOE staff job as a captain). All of the company commanders also had previously served as platoon leader in a new unit—frequently twice. Furthermore, almost all officers entering a new-unit XO/S3 position have already served as company commander in a new unit. Many of them have also previously been an XO/S3 (though sometimes in an old unit).

Among old-unit paths, the picture is a little more mixed but still provides fairly intense preparation for leaders. An officer who becomes a company commander in an old unit usually has two platoon leadership jobs under his belt; often he has also had a TOE assignment as a captain. An officer who becomes an XO/S3 always has a TOE company command in his background, and more than half have also had an enhanced assignment as a captain (paths 5, 10, and 12).

Finally, this solution has the overall effect of stacking up leadership experience in successive assignments. It produces a considerable number of officers who have served twice as platoon leaders, then as TOE company commander, and then as XO/S3. Moreover, almost all of those who reach XO/S3 also have further operational preparation for future leadership: either (1) a second XO/S3 assignment or (2) an enhanced assignment at O-4.

Notice, however, that this system still places about 30 percent of entrants on paths (number 14 and 15) that serve exclusively in the TDA after their first assignment at O-3, with no leadership assignment after O-2. Again, this channeling of some officers into a "TDA track" is a necessary consequence of the concentration of operational experience in the other paths that we just discussed.

We do observe that the preparation of new-unit commanders could be better. In path 6, for example, officers serve two back-to-back assignments as XO/S3 in new units, but their previous preparation was largely in old units. Most of the other paths culminating in new-unit XO/S3 also contain preceding old-unit assignments. If one placed very great value on developing a cadre of leaders with deep experience in the new environment, it might be more attractive to stack up repeated new-unit tours, one after another. So we asked: Is that possible, as a limiting condition?

Maximizing Repetitive New-Unit Experience

Table 4.11 shows the result if we specify greater preferences for repetitive experiences in new units. To implement those preferences, we examined the set of paths that contained assignments to new units. Within that set, we then identified those paths that had multiple new-unit assignments, when the path culminated in a leadership job in a new unit. An example would be a path containing these assignments: (1) new-unit PL; (2) another assignment as new-unit PL; (3) new-unit company commander; (4) new-unit XO. For such repetitive paths, we added incremental points to reflect the potential value of having a cadre of officers who were well-grounded in new unit operations.

The result in Table 4.11 confirms that it is feasible to achieve such repetitive assignments. Path 2 concentrates new-unit experience in a small set of officers who have essentially the ultimate degree of specialization: they get two tours as platoon leader, two tours as company commander, and two tours as XO/S3, all in new units. In addition, they get the added benefit of one TOE assignment in a new unit as a

Table 4.11
Maximizing Repetitive Assignments to New Units

Path	No. of Entrants	O-2		O-3			O-4		
1	2	PL	PL	TOE	CDR	INST	TOE	XO/S3	INST
2	14	PL	PL	TOE	CDR	CDR	TOE	XO/S3	XO/S3
3	1	PL	PL	TOE	CDR	ENH	TOE	XO/S3	XO/S3
4	12	PL	PL	TOE	CDR	ENH	INST	XO/S3	ENH
5	11	PL	PL	TOE	CDR	INST	TOE	XO/S3	INST
6	1	PL	PL	TOE	CDR	ENH	TOE	XO/S3	XO/S3
7	1	PL	TOE	TOE	INST	INST	TOE	INST	INST
8	33	PL	PL	TOE	CDR	INST	TOE	XO/S3	ENH
9	33	PL	PL	TOE	CDR	INST	INST	XO/S3	XO/S3
10	3	PL	PL	TOE	CDR	ENH	TOE	XO/S3	ENH
11	97	PL	PL	TOE	CDR	ENH	INST	XO/S3	ENH
12	51	PL	TOE	TOE	INST	INST	INST	INST	INST
13	14	PL	INST	TOE	INST	INST	TOE	INST	INST
14	30	PL	INST	INST	INST	INST	INST	INST	INST

captain. They also cover the lion's share of all new-unit XO/S3 positions; only two other paths, both containing only one entrant, culminate in new-unit XO/S3 (paths 3 and 6).

This stacking of one new-unit job after another would undoubtedly build a great deal of specialized expertise among officers in new units. Every officer who became a new-unit company commander or XO/S3 would eventually serve a second tour in that same leadership job, enabling him to build directly on his previous and most recent experience.

The other side of the coin, however, might be viewed as a drawback. In the system of Table 4.11, few officers move between new and old units. The largest paths (8–9 and 11–15) consist entirely of assignments to old units and TDA organizations. The effect is to build up two quite distinct officer corps, with relatively few persons who move between them. For example, just a few small paths (1, 4, and 5) produce an XO/S3 in an old unit who has any experience at all in a new unit; they account for only 13 percent of all officers who eventually become an old-unit XO/S3. None of them has previous experience commanding a company in a new unit. Thus, the leaders of old units would have little personal experience in the new world, and they might not be well equipped to interact with or take advantage of the emergent capabilities of new units. They might also be unprepared to deal with new missions if their "old" organization were suddenly tasked to do so. Therefore, although it is possible to push the system to the extreme represented by Table 4.11, the Army would need to weigh its benefits in terms of specialized new-unit expertise against the concomitant downsides and risks. In essence, this is another case where the Army can obtain depth (new-unit expertise) only by sacrificing some breadth (interchange of people between the two types of units).

Increasing the Number of New Units

The above analysis shows that the Army can provide leaders with high levels of operational experience when the number of new units is relatively small (about 12 percent of total officer authorizations). But what happens if there are more new units? The special demands of new units could grow more widespread if an increasing fraction of the force pursued new missions, or if transformation affected an increasing number of units.

To address this question, we decided to experiment with *tripling the number of new units*. To do that, we reallocated positions from old to new units in inputs to the model, producing a new personnel structure that had three times as many new positions as in the preceding analyses. However, for this excursion we returned to the preference scheme used for Table 4.10: that is, we discarded the intense preferences for repeated new-unit assignments that we analyzed immediately above. The resulting paths for this excursion are shown in Table 4.12.

Under these circumstances, Army officers can still succeed in getting a great deal of experience, as indicated by the successive patterns of TOE leadership and staff segments shown in the larger paths (e.g., paths 1, 3, 6, 8, and 11). Because there are now so many new units, many more paths contain new-unit segments. Career paths often mix new and old experience, which provides more breadth for many officers. For example, on path 1 (a large path) the officers serve numerous assignments in new units, including company command, but end up serving as XO/S3 in an old unit. On path 3, the reverse occurs: the officers get new-unit experience in platoons, then old-unit experience in TOE and company command, and then serve back-to-back tours as XO/S3 in new units. Also, enhanced positions now receive a mixture of people with old and new experience, compared with Table 4.11, where the dearth of new-unit positions meant that most officers entering enhanced jobs had experience only in old units.

Of course, because old units still account for the majority of positions, a large number of officers still serve their entire career in old units (i.e., paths 11–15, including about 60 percent of all entrants). And, because of the demand for TDA institutional positions, it is still true that nearly one-third of all entrants follow paths that keep them in the TDA Army for most of their career. Overall, though, this scheme provides a reasonable degree of experience of both types for most key positions. We certainly do not observe any general breakdown in the system as the number of new units grows.

Table 4.12
Assignment Sequences: Triple New Units

Path	No. of Entrants	O-2		O-3			O-4		
1	53	PL	PL	TOE	CDR	ENH	INST	XO/S3	ENH
2	2	PL	PL	TOE	CDR	ENH	INST	XO/S3	ENH
3	24	PL	PL	TOE	CDR	ENH	INST	XO/S3	XO/S3
4	5	PL	PL	INST	CDR	CDR	INST	XO/S3	XO/S3
5	9	PL	PL	TOE	CDR	CDR	INST	XO/S3	XO/S3
6	12	PL	PL	TOE	CDR	ENH	INST	XO/S3	XO/S3
7	1	PL	PL	TOE	CDR	ENH	INST	XO/S3	ENH
8	13	PL	PL	INST	CDR	ENH	INST	XO/S3	ENH
9	2	PL	TOE	TOE	INST	INST	TOE	INST	INST
10	2	PL	TOE	TOE	INST	INST	TOE	INST	INST
11	67	PL	PL	TOE	CDR	INST	TOE	XO/S3	ENH
12	8	PL	PL	TOE	CDR	ENH	TOE	XO/S3	ENH
13	12	PL	PL	INST	CDR	INST	INST	XO/S3	INST
14	47	PL	TOE	TOE	INST	INST	INST	INST	INST
15	44	PL	INST	TOE	INST	INST	INST	INST	INST

Requiring More Senior Grades for New-Unit Leadership

As a final excursion, we decided to consider a marked departure from past practice, namely requiring officers to become much more senior before they are given leadership roles. The premise was a scenario such as this: Suppose that the demands of new units become so varied and so intense that young officers simply cannot cope with the breadth of responsibilities at an early stage of their career. In our interviews with commanders and officials, we sometimes heard this possibility broached. Some would argue, for example, that the job of company commander is becoming so multifaceted that it cannot be handled by a junior officer with, say, five years of experience. According to this view, leaders may need many more years of experience under their belt before they can truly master the skills needed. In support of this view, one can recall the large number of skills and subskills demanded by the contemporary environment, discussed in Chapter Three, and the demanding intellectual quality of recognitional decision making, discussed in Chapter Two.

Without passing judgment on the current validity of that hypothesis, we wanted to explore the system's ability to respond to it if it should be true (or become true in the future). So we decided to see what would happen if the Army stipulated that leaders in new units needed to be much more senior, by requiring that:

- Only a captain could fill a position of platoon leader in a new unit.
- Only a major could fill a position of company commander in a new unit.

Table 4.13 shows the resulting set of paths for a system operating under those constraints and attempting to fill the baseline position structure.

When we began to examine this structure, we were unsure that any solution would be feasible. However, the model did find a feasible solution based on our point score calculations. Notice that in this system, the position of platoon leader in a new unit ("PL" shown in heavy white type) appears only at the grade of O-3.[31] Similarly, the position of commander in a new unit ("CDR" in heavy white type) appears only at the grade of O-4.

Because of the position structure, this system leads to a remarkable degree of concentration in new-unit experience. Every company commander in a new unit has already served as a new-unit platoon leader, and every XO/S3 in a new unit has previously served in new units as both platoon leader and company commander. Thus, instituting these seniority constraints creates a high degree of specialization in the

Table 4.13
O-4s as Company Commanders and O-3s as Platoon Leaders in New Units

Path	No. of Entrants	O-2		O-3			O-4		
1	24	PL	PL	TOE	CDR	CDR	TOE	XO/S3	ENH
2	11	PL	PL	TOE	CDR	CDR	TOE	XO/S3	XO/S3
3	1	PL	TOE	TOE	TOE	TOE	INST	INST	INST
4	35	PL	TOE	TOE	TOE	TOE	INST	INST	INST
5	13	PL	TOE	TOE	CDR	INST	TOE	XO/S3	ENH
6	3	PL	TOE	TOE	CDR	CDR	INST	XO/S3	XO/S3
7	59	PL	INST	TOE	INST	INST	INST	INST	INST
8	17	PL	INST	TOE	CDR	INST	INST	XO/S3	ENH
9	8	PL	INST	TOE	CDR	CDR	TOE	XO/S3	ENH
10	10	PL	INST	TOE	CDR	CDR	TOE	XO/S3	XO/S3
11	6	PL	INST	TOE	CDR	CDR	INST	INST	INST
12	13	PL	INST	TOE	CDR	ENH	TOE	XO/S3	ENH
13	25	PL	PL	PL	ENH	CDR	INST	XO/S3	ENH
14	44	PL	PL	PL	ENH	INST	CDR	XO/S3	ENH
15	32	PL	PL	PL	ENH	INST	CDR	XO/S3	XO/S3

[31] Because these platoon leaders are now captains, we did not require them to wait until their second assignment as an O-3 to become a platoon leader, as we had done in the earlier runs.

force, reserving a minority of officers for new-unit jobs and keeping the others in old units. It also means that O-4 enhanced jobs are never filled by an officer who has new-unit experience as XO or S3; all of those enhanced jobs are filled by officers who were previously XO or S3 in an old unit.

Implications

Achievable Levels of Operational Experience

Overall, the results of this chapter are encouraging in that they highlight feasible career paths that produce in-depth operational experience for every condition that we specified. The Army has latitude, therefore, to provide its leaders more time in field units and more exposure to operational positions, if it needs to do so. Within the constraints of the current position structure, it is possible to ensure that many officers get repeated assignments that would imbue operational expertise, including TOE leadership, TOE staff, and enhanced positions.

Moreover, we found that the Army could build repetitive experience in *new* units, even to the point of developing a cadre of officers who get sequential leadership assignments in new units at the grades of lieutenant, captain, and major. In most of the solutions found by the model, those same officers spend the great majority of their time in operational assignments, or in TDA enhanced assignments. Thus, they get a concentrated career of experience in operational environments at all echelons.

It is clearly possible, therefore, to create considerable depth of operational experience. The downside is a reduction in breadth: under most of these assignment programs, the officer corps becomes specialized in several ways. First, while some officers proceed on an intense operational track as described above, other officers—in fact, a sizable group—move along a separate track within the TDA institutional Army after just two or three early TOE assignments. Second, if the Army desires some officers to have depth in new-unit assignments, most others will see sequential assignments in old units; few officers move between the two.

These results thus cut two ways. While they produce a group of officers with high operational expertise, those same officers lack much exposure to the Army's TDA institutions or other environments. Eventually the Army would have a cohort of leaders with only a bare modicum of experience in the non-operational world. In a word, they would be narrow. The opposite applies to officers serving in TDA assignments: While such an officer typically gets two TOE assignments as a platoon leader and/or a staff officer as a captain, he lacks further TOE experience as a captain or major. If one believes that it is important, for example, for a major in a TDA job to have TOE company command experience, that would be precluded in those instances where we modeled repetitive TOE assignments to concentrate on building depth of operational expertise for a smaller set of officers.

All of these arguments apply equally to the distinction between new and old positions. To the degree that the system develops some officers with great depth in new-unit operations, it also creates another group of officers with little or no experience in new units. We have seen directly that this picture can become fairly stark, creating two groups that are largely different, and also isolated from each other.

Providing More Opportunities to Gain Operational Experience

The above results highlight a dilemma: Experience in units can be increased for some officers, but only by reducing it for others. Therefore the Army is likely to seek other options if it decides that it needs higher levels of operational experience for many officers, especially in new units. While it is too soon to know whether this may be necessary, we can anticipate some key policy or structural changes that are likely to be advocated (indeed, some of these ideas arose in our discussions with senior officers and officials).

One course of action—often advocated by operators—is to increase the availability of officers for operational assignments. Many observers, for example, have proposed reducing the number of positions in the institutional TDA. If the Army's uniformed strength remained constant, officers would thereby be freed to spend more time in TOE units.[32] This would increase the supply of officers but would also carry additional costs to provide that supply. For example, reducing the number of uniformed officers in the TDA would require additional funds because the same TDA functions would still need to be performed, perhaps by Army civilians or contract organizations. The persons actually performing the work might be retired Army personnel, as has been the case in some related programs.[33] However accomplished, the Army would realistically still need to pay for the work, and therefore its budget would need to rise to recognize the costs.

However, a problem with such actions is that they do not actually provide more *positions* that offer operational experience. Suppose, for example, that officers are removed from the TDA and made available to TOE units. Where will they be placed? If they move into existing TOE positions, others who would have occupied those positions will be displaced. More generally, if the number of positions in TOE units remains the same, the number of officers who can pursue operationally intensive de-

[32] A variant of this would be to seek to lengthen officer careers, so that each officer produces more man-years during a career, or simply to increase the number of officers in the inventory.

[33] See, for example, Goldman et al. (1999).

velopmental paths also remains the same.[34] The only way to expand aggregate opportunity for operational experience is to increase the number of TOE positions (or TDA enhanced positions, in our analysis).

Therefore, to pursue this course, the Army would also need to increase the number of positions in the TOE. Such a change would have to be supported by an argument that TOE units need more uniformed officers, for instance to support emerging missions.[35] For example, Army units may need more officers to conduct 24-hour operations, to sustain split-base operations (where part of the unit is deployed and the rest remains at home station), or to carry out extensive planning for multiple, high-tempo deployments.[36] Under these circumstances, converting TDA positions to TOE would meet additional requirements *and* give the officer corps greater experience in operational units.

An alternative approach is to provide officers with broader operational expertise through venues other than assignments in units. The obvious candidates would be Army and other defense schools, and assignments to joint or interagency positions. In such non-unit venues an officer could be exposed to a wider array of situations and gain a more varied base of knowledge and experience. Longer careers could make this option more feasible by making it possible for individuals to deepen their operational skills *and* to have more diverse experiences, which could enhance their adaptability. Apart from the effects on an individual, this would create a broader base of experience in the officer corps, providing a greater range of backgrounds that the Army can tap when necessary. We will explore these possibilities in the next chapter.

---

[34] This is true whenever the number of officers in the inventory is the same as the required number, as we assumed in our analysis. On the other hand, if inventory is not large enough to fill requirements, then of course there is benefit in increasing it until it matches demand. Above that level, the argument above applies.

[35] It is conceivable that the Army would add new unit structure and thereby add new positions, but it seems unlikely that such an expansion could be justified on the grounds of needing entire new units simply to develop leaders more intensively.

[36] See Sortor and Polich (2001) for examples of the ways in which higher-tempo conditions place particular stress on staffs in units from battalion through division.

CHAPTER FIVE

Balancing Breadth and Depth

In the past, the pre-eminent venue for developing leaders has been the operational assignment in a unit. The analysis in Chapter Four has shown, reassuringly, that the Army will continue to be able to afford its leaders a great deal of this form of operational experience. However, there are limits to this reliance on direct experience in units. As we saw in Chapter Four, significantly increasing the amount of operational experience that leaders get in new missions or units could result in an unpalatable degree of specialization: The pool of future leaders would be divided into one group with significant experience in such missions or units, and another group with little or none. Thus, operational depth would be purchased at the expense of breadth within the officer corps.

Would it be wise to foster this degree of specialization, including the resulting narrowness in officers' background? Or are there countervailing imperatives that argue in the direction of *breadth*—attempting to give all officers a wider background spanning operations, Army institutions, and experiences outside the Army?

This chapter addresses those questions, arguing that breadth deserves its due alongside depth. In doing so, it also raises and addresses a second question: How might the Army encourage officer breadth while still enhancing operational skills? We outline ways in which officer time spent in non-operational venues, such as institutional positions and non-Army assignments, might be used for both aims: rounding out operational abilities and providing broadening experiences.

The following discussion is organized around three important arguments in favor of breadth: (1) the proliferation of *specific operational skills* needed in an uncertain environment, (2) *intellectual and cognitive abilities* needed to support rapid, recognitional decision making in a fluid situation, and (3) a wide range of *cultural knowledge and perspective* needed for effective performance in unfamiliar, nonmilitary and non-U.S. locales.

Specific Operational Skills

Proliferation of Skill Requirements

Because of more varied missions and situations, officers now face a longer list of skills and abilities to be developed, as outlined in Chapter Three. Mastering the entire list is a tall order, especially given the large number of functions that officers must already be prepared to perform.

These skills are also complex, incorporating many contributing or enabling subtasks and numerous variations in the circumstances and conditions in which they are needed. For example, consider the following brief but illustrative listing of subtasks for one of our key skill areas, "force protection."[1]

- Maintain local security at traffic control points;
- Conduct convoy security missions;
- Conduct raids in urban environments to capture suspected enemy;
- Properly identify and engage hostile targets in an urban environment;
- Execute actions on contact for ambush in restrictive terrain;
- Collect and use human intelligence about enemy forces;
- Conduct intelligence analysis of convoy routes, patrol routes, and checkpoint locations.

The other skill areas exhibit a similar degree of complexity.

Of course, traditional military practice would favor training all of these skills in unit settings. However, the more time that future leaders spend in units honing their operational skills, the less time they will spend directing Army institutions, serving in joint positions, obtaining military or civilian education, and so forth. In turn, that would limit the background of battalion and brigade commanders, who need perspective on more general matters of strategy and doctrine, as well as knowledge of how the Army operates as an institution.

Moreover, the most senior officer positions require considerable breadth, including familiarity with institutions not only in the Army but also in other services, other U.S. government agencies, and international organizations. Paradoxically, a large majority of officers serving in senior positions—including general officers—are traditionally selected from the pool of younger leaders with the greatest operational experience. If the strongest candidates for promotion have a narrow background, the result—in a few years time—will be senior officers who likewise have narrow back-

[1] This list is incomplete and illustrative only. However, it demonstrates how a skill that may seem straightforward can represent a wide range of different activities that themselves can be complex. To further this point, we invite the reader to envision the subtasks under "understand and employ the capabilities of combined arms and joint forces . . ."

grounds. Therefore, the Army faces limits on the degree to which it could channel junior leaders into operational assignments, thereby depriving them of broadening experiences in other assignments.[2]

Prioritizing Skills and Selecting Development Venues

Given this tension between breadth and depth, how can the Army develop the most important operational skills and provide at least some exposure to all of the skills that may be needed? To make choices and achieve balance, we recommend two steps. First, the Army should review recent operations—going back at least to Somalia—to assess the performance of junior leaders and determine which skill areas constitute the highest-priority needs. Such a review could proceed from a checklist such as the nine skill areas that we have identified, and involve after-action reviews, "lessons learned" documents, interviews with commanders and participants, and so forth. Reports and lessons learned documents from Afghanistan and Iraq indicate a significant degree of innovation on the part of Army leaders at even the lowest levels; capturing both the training and education implications in this material will pay large dividends.[3]

Second, the Army needs a set of priorities to choose which skill areas get the most attention, and a mechanism for allocating different education and training "venues" to the various skills. Our view of priorities was offered at the end of Chapter Three: Top priority should go to skills associated with force protection, joint and combined arms operations, and civilians on the battlefield.

We would then use these priorities to assign skills to a set of desired proficiency levels such as these:[4]

---

[2] Recent unpublished RAND research has indicated that senior leadership positions typically require significant expertise in many broad areas, well beyond the nine skill areas listed in Table 3.1 in Chapter Three. Numerous senior officers told us that a lack of breadth in their background was the most formidable problem they had to overcome in their current job.

[3] Among public sources, useful summaries can be found in the work of Cordesman (e.g., *The Lessons of Afghanistan*, 2002). Jones et al. (2005) and Dobbins et al. (2005) provide longer and wider perspectives. Innovation and adaptation are also strong themes running through the Army's lessons learned and after-action reports. Fontenot, Degen, and Tohn (2004) provide a detailed and unclassified account of the operation in Iraq. For those with access, the Center for Army Lessons Learned (Fort Leavenworth, Kansas) maintains extensive holdings related to ground operations, focused generally on operational experience and innovations.

[4] Readers familiar with the educational literature will recognize that this classification is loosely related to the well-known categorization known as "Bloom's taxonomy," which posits a series of similar proficiency levels ranging from knowledge through comprehension, application, analysis, synthesis, and evaluation. Our classification titles attempt to correspond to military concepts, but they parallel Bloom except at the highest level, where we combined his top two categories into one. Cf. Bloom (1956). Numerous Internet websites have informative expositions of Bloom's taxonomy. We are indebted to John Lewis of Cubic, Inc. for first suggesting to us the applicability of Bloom's taxonomy in the examination of military leader skills. Also see in particular Cubic (2003).

- **Information only.** Knowledge and familiarity, typically conveyed in the classroom.
- **Information with some practice.** Knowledge supplemented by, say, simulation experience.
- **Competence with some practice.** Ability developed through additional exposure, such as practice in field-unit training. May require more practice—"just-in-time training" or a Mission Readiness Exercise (MRE)—before commitment to an operational mission.
- **High confidence in most scenarios.** Having operational experience in applying the skill.
- **Second-nature execution.** Extensive operational experience or accumulation of numerous training and educational experiences.[5]

Figure 5.1 shows one way in which we might decide which skill areas should receive particular attention and which development methods are most appropriate. The upper panel in the figure exhibits the five proficiency levels just discussed. The row labeled "skill area" shows how we would map the nine leader skill areas onto the range of proficiency levels, based on our discussions in Chapter Three regarding the importance of these skill areas relative to one another. The horizontal ranges in various rows represent levels of proficiency that we would suggest as minimum goals for each skill area.

The lower panel in Figure 5.1, containing the rows labeled "development method" and "development venue," illustrates the types of experiences and locales—classroom, simulation, unit experience—that correspond to each proficiency level. For example, we called out three skills as most critical: joint and combined operations, force protection, and interacting with civilians on the battlefield. Accordingly, in these areas one would prefer leaders to attain the highest level of proficiency, second-nature execution.

The figure suggests that the highest proficiency level would be developed through a combination of institutional education, individual efforts, and multiple

---

[5] We could also describe this level as "fully developed ability to envision circumstances and make appropriate and timely decisions," to indicate the close relationship between this level of proficiency and the overarching competencies of situational understanding and recognitional decision making. As we have mentioned, "second-nature execution" is similar to what Army leadership doctrine refers to as "intuition." For further discussion of intuition in the context of recognitional decision making, see Klein (1998) and our discussion in Chapter Two. Klein defines intuition as "the use of experience to recognize key patterns that indicate the dynamics of the situation" and observes that depth of experience will allow a decision maker to "recognize things without knowing how we do the recognizing." Figure 5.1 captures the concept by requiring significant operational experience at each level. Note also the implied confluence of situational understanding ("recognize . . . the dynamics of the situation") and the ability to make good "intuitive" decisions.

Figure 5.1
Leader Proficiency Levels

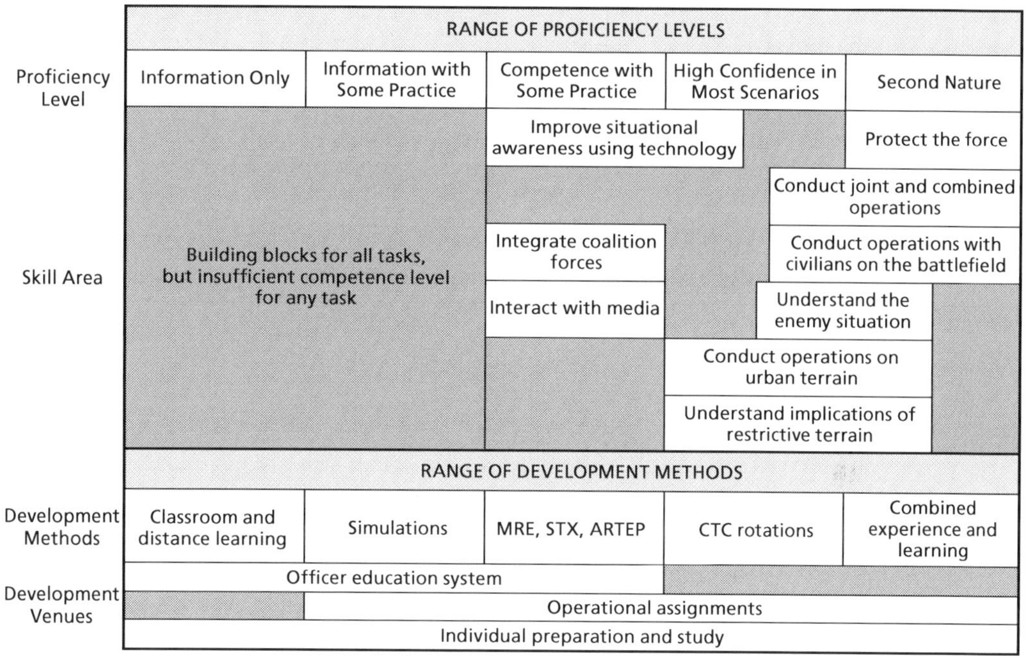

RAND *MG281-5.1*

operational or training experiences.[6] This is consistent with the widely held view that many skills need continuous development and repetition to develop through a cumulative sequence of proficiency levels. The foundation is a sound education in fundamentals—making education an essential precursor. Understanding of the fundamentals can later be reinforced by experience in applying them in operational settings, actual or realistically simulated. Later educational assignments allow the leader an opportunity for reflecting on previous experiences, sharing in others' experiences, and developing intellectual curiosity.

While different observers may ascribe different priorities to these operational skills, it seems essential to have some such method to circumvent the tendency for all aspects of leader development to demand equal emphasis.

---

[6] Notice that the lowest levels of proficiency, appearing on the left side of the diagram, form a basis for building competency, but they are viewed here as not adequate for any of the skill areas under consideration. This view—emphasizing thorough grounding in fundamentals—was confirmed throughout our discussions with Army officials, civilian and military, in both academic and field training environments.

Using the Army's Institutions for Leverage

It will be difficult to develop all of these skills at the same time. Because many other requirements compete for attention and time, there is a danger that any new requirements, however critical, will get short shrift. How, then, might the Army act to ensure that these high-priority skills get the attention they deserve? Here we suggest a general strategy that relies on the strength of the Army's existing institutions.

Foundations in school curricula. From the basic officer course through the war college, Army professional education curricula should emphasize skills that are particularly relevant in the contemporary environment. Providing this foundation ensures a basic level of knowledge and proficiency throughout the force. It also gives commanders assurance about the basic preparation of junior leaders and ensures some degree of standardization and uniform terminology as units scramble to prepare for newly identified missions.

Distributed learning. Distributed learning (DL) and related technologies can help, not only to carry "academic" material to the field but also to capture current operational material from actual operations and from training exercises. This new material can then be brought into discussions in academic environments, supplementing and illustrating the relevance of the fundamentals and bringing them to life in current operational contexts.

The first of these ideas—using DL to funnel educational material to the field—has gotten more attention, but it is important not to overstate its potential payoffs. As we have argued elsewhere (Leonard et al., 2001), there are several limitations in using DL, chief among them limitations on leader time. Particularly in today's environment, leaders in units have little time for formalized academic pursuits. If anything, they are more likely to use DL as part of self-development or preparation for upcoming missions. For example, DL could provide leaders with a more accessible and usable mechanism to recall things that were learned earlier or to capitalize on things learned elsewhere by leaders in similar situations. This could help reduce the time needed for them to gain proficiency in their new positions. It will also directly bolster confidence for leaders to know they can have ready access to the key lessons learned from others in similar circumstances.[7]

CTC rotations. The Army's Combat Training Centers (CTCs) conduct exercises that constitute the central training event for most units. CTCs also feature experienced observer-controllers as arbiters of after-action reviews that spotlight areas of difficulty and suggest methods for improvement. Thus, the CTCs are in a position to

---

[7] This is not to suggest that lessons from other places and times will always be relevant, or that leaders will always have time to access these lessons under the time pressures of their current situation. Rather, we suggest that better access to a broad array of lessons learned under similar circumstances will enable leaders periodically to enrich their background knowledge of *possible* situations and what kinds of solutions do and do not work. Thus, as we will argue later in this chapter, learning technologies have potential to help leaders master the general intellectual abilities they will need, as well as specific operational skills.

influence the agenda and standards for all unit training. CTCs should review their scenarios and training plans to consider whether the key leader skills that we have identified are getting necessary attention and how units' CTC rotations can enhance those skills.

Support for home-station simulations and exercises. Unit exercises and their use of simulations vary widely in their focus and content. Support from Army institutions (particularly training development) could help to ensure that units are aware of key skills needed in the contemporary operational environment and help them adapt exercises to practice those skills. In a time of great change and high operational pace, such as the present, units are not likely to have the time or resources to devote to new training initiatives. The institutional Army should help perform this function and should have resources available to make it happen.

Capture data on skill training and execution. Through mechanisms such as those above, the Army might integrate institutional support more closely with unit operations. As part of this integration, the Army could also capture and analyze data on what skills were trained and executed in unit activities at home station, at CTCs, and perhaps even while deployed. Having such data would convey many benefits; for example, it could make it possible for key lessons to be shared throughout the operating force *and* with those responsible for development of training and educational programs. It would also make it easier for each unit, and the operational Army as a whole, to focus simulations and other exercises to re-emphasize weak areas or areas where skills decay quickly. This in turn would help in the design of CTC scenarios and MREs.

Such initiatives would help knit together more closely the processes of training and curriculum development, the delivery of training and educational products, and the gathering of feedback on the effects of the products. Such enhanced connections would aid leader development in two ways: directly, in developing current leaders; and indirectly, through building and refining an institutional base of knowledge regarding what skills are needed and what ways work best to imbue leaders with those skills.

Intellectual and Cognitive Abilities

A second argument for fostering breadth in Army officers stems from the importance of higher-level intellectual and cognitive abilities in the modern environment. As documented earlier in this report, today's conditions require leaders to make decisions more quickly, in unfamiliar situations amid ambiguity and uncertainty. To do so, officers need to be facile in "recognitional" decision making, which itself requires abstract intellectual abilities backed up by a broad background of experience and knowledge.

Recognitional Decision Making

What are these higher-level abilities, and how can they be developed? As we discussed in Chapter Two, modern empirical research reveals that leaders making decisions under stress (such as firefighters, police, emergency physicians, and military commanders) typically use an abbreviated and intuitive approach rooted in their own experience, rather than considering all options and formally evaluating them. This process, described as recognitional decision making,[8] relies on several attributes and abilities: pattern recognition, perceptual acuity, mental simulation, critical thinking, adaptability, and above all breadth of experience.[9]

As we synthesized the process, the decision maker sorts through his base of past experience and knowledge, seeking a model whose attributes resemble the situation that he now confronts. He then mentally simulates one or more courses of action to assess their possible outcomes, given the situation as he understands it. All of these skills rest critically on one's base of knowledge and experience, and they are typically developed by practice across a variety of situations. If the range of experience is too narrow, the model may be inappropriate, the forecast of outcomes may be incorrect, and the resulting action may fail or backfire.

Education: A Key Venue for Developing Decision-Making Abilities

The above cluster of abilities differs from the operational skills that we outlined earlier in one key respect: they are inherently *cognitive* processes, modes of thinking. As such, they are better suited to development in an academic institutional setting rather than in an action-oriented field unit. These abilities require reflection on past experience, ferreting out the essential elements of a new problem, entertaining alternatives, and thinking through the consequences of actions that have not yet been taken. Such intellectual endeavors are well suited to the measured pace and reflective environment of an academic institution.

Moreover, once learned, these abilities need to be exercised in a wide range of different situations—not just repeated, but applied in varying circumstances and locales. This exercise process may be likened to working problems in mathematics, as a new concept or method is applied successively in different contexts and to solve "harder" problems. Such a variety of problems could never be "worked" in a unit en-

---

[8] As we have noted previously, approximate synonyms used by other authors include "heuristic," "intuitive," or "naturalistic" decision making. Klein (1998) describes this as naturalistic because his model of the process was derived from observation of actual decision making in natural contexts rather than in specially designed experiments.

[9] Recognizing the importance of such abilities, the Army has adapted its doctrine to emphasize lifelong learning and higher-level meta-competencies such as adaptability and "self-awareness" (U.S. Army Training and Doctrine Command, Army Training and Leader Development Panel, 2001). Army educators and trainers concluded that it is impossible to anticipate all the varied features of future scenarios and hence to master, in advance, all the skills that will be needed. Instead, it is hoped, officers who possess these more general, higher-level faculties will be able to quickly master new material and manage new situations.

vironment; there would be too many scenarios to consider, and they would consume the time and resources of entire units as the leader experimented with different possible solutions.[10]

Of course, such difficult intellectual skills are not apt to be mastered in a single course or school. In many fields, students are expected to need repeated exposure to complex concepts and methods before reaching a mature understanding.[11] And much of what we are considering—critical thinking, mental simulation, and recognition of relevant features of the situation—is particularly challenging. In civilian education, for example, high-level critical faculties and a detached, hypothesis-testing orientation are generally developed only at the graduate level. Therefore, the Army should expect that these topics need to be revisited in each educational module, from the basic officer course through the war college level.

Are such investments worth it? We argue a definite "yes," not only because these skills yield better and faster decisions, but also because the skills generalize across a multitude of domains. Critical thinking, for example, can be learned in one area but applied to many others.[12] This suggests that *any* education regime that inculcates critical thinking—including civilian education—will contribute to developing the critical thinking skills needed by Army leaders.

Steps to Enhance Decision Skills

Army schools. A first step is to develop more educational modules that specifically center on recognitional decision making and its supporting skills—critical thinking and evaluation, identifying key aspects of ambiguous and uncertain situations, comparing them with other situations and past experience, conducting mental simulations of alternative actions, and assessing possible outcomes. The material should cover both the logic and method of recognitional decision making—including examples of how concrete decisions are actually made in high-stress situations.

---

[10] Naturally, operational experience in units still plays a crucial role. However, such experience will be more valuable if applied in a way that refines skills that can be taught in other venues, and some of the relevant forms of experience in critical thinking can be afforded without tying up the resources of entire units.

[11] For example, development of "mathematical maturity" is often said to require time and exposure in several courses. For a relevant military example, see the discussion of critical thinking in Cannon-Bowers and Salas (2000), where it is argued that training in critical thinking produces some effects quickly but is more effective when done at intervals over time.

[12] For a discussion of transferability, see Cannon-Bowers and Salas, (2000) pp. 185–188, which grew out of a project done for the U.S. Navy focusing on "tactical decision making under stress." While Navy tactical (and operational) decisions differ in many ways from those that Army leaders confront, we argue that the critical thinking abilities underpinning them are quite similar if not identical. This work includes a full chapter on "critical thinking," which, as we have stated previously, we interpret as synonymous with the term "critical reasoning." "Critical reasoning," of course, also appears as a key ability in official Army leadership doctrine and was frequently mentioned in our interviews with commanders and academic officials.

Such modules should appear in the curricula in all Army schools and leader education programs. In our view this would include not only the branch schools, but also the Command and General Staff College, the War College, and other more specialized institutions that educate field-grade officers.

Practical exercise tools. It is widely recognized that complex skills are more readily mastered if abstract concepts are supplemented by illustrative scenarios, vignettes, and practical exercises. Many courses already use practicums with scenarios that address concrete problems, such as the group of interrelated scenarios used in Intermediate Level Education at the Command and General Staff College. Such exercises can be enhanced if they include access to simulations (automated or not) that portray locations, resources, civilian populations and infrastructure, and the other features of the contemporary environment that pose difficult challenges.

Distributed learning. An additional advantage of developing practical problems and simulations is that they can then be used in non-academic settings. For example, such tools could be used by leaders to accomplish refresher or familiarization training as part of predeployment preparations. They could also be used for self-study by individuals, and possibly for support to command post exercises in units. Such tools can challenge the user to consider a variety of situations and think through their implications, thus avoiding premature focus on a single-point estimate of a future mission or a single-point solution.

CTC rotations could also make use of tools such as the simulations, vignettes, and scenarios mentioned above. The CTC's standard after-action review would be an effective vehicle for reinforcement. CTC trainers are ideally positioned to engage leaders in examination of these skills and their operational implications; all we spoke to would be eager to do so.

We note, however, that officers in units need *dedicated time* to study and develop their skills if distributed learning is to achieve much effect. Even in peacetime environments, leaders with unit responsibilities have scant time for other pursuits; in the current high-tempo situation, it is unrealistic to expect that leaders will be able to get such time (or that hard-pressed commanders will permit it). This constraint is part of the reason that we will argue, later in this chapter, for an increase in the number of officers so that such longer-term investments can be made.

Graduate education. Such complex skills are not likely to be mastered in an undergraduate curriculum or a few short courses thereafter. We argue that the Army, like civilian employers, should recognize the value of graduate education in external institutions. Civilian graduate school can provide in-depth education in logic, analysis, hypothesis testing, and critical evaluation of evidence—all key elements of recognitional decision making. Such education also will broaden officers' perspectives, exposing them to alternative ways of thinking and the latest information and research, all of which will enhance adaptation to new environments. The Army could seek advanced education for its officers just for the value of that education in broadening perspectives and developing reasoning skills.[13]

Such a policy would stand in marked contrast to recent practice, which for financial reasons has required a one-for-one correspondence between a period of "advanced civil schooling" and a "utilization tour" following that schooling. Loosening that restriction would consume more money for school expenses and more time within officers' careers. This is needed, however, to counter a perverse situation that has arisen under the current management system. Under current practices, most officers attending graduate programs come from the specialized career fields. Few officers in the operations career field obtain Army-sponsored graduate-level education in civilian institutions, even though operators are more likely to make the most far-reaching decisions in the near term and to constitute the majority of the Army's senior leaders in the long term.

Although ameliorating this situation would impose costs, it would also yield other benefits. For example, wider opportunities for graduate-level education could serve as a retention incentive, helping to keep capable officers in the Army.[14] The result could be an officer corps with more stability and continuity—fewer officers entering and leaving the force—which in turn would cut costs for recruiting, educating, and training new officers each year. In addition, we argue that a well-educated officer corps will be more effective in communicating with peers in civilian institutions—thus fostering civil-military integration—and more effective in interactions with external elites (such as officials and staff members elsewhere in the defense establishment and in the legislative branch).

Breadth of Cultural Knowledge and Perspective

Perspective Beyond the Army

A third and profound aspect of breadth is familiarity with external (non-Army) institutions. These institutions run the gamut from military partners (e.g., other services and joint organizations) to other U.S. government agencies and international entities such as NATO, the United Nations, and allied coalitions. Knowing about these external institutions helps to coordinate and plan operations, but that is not all. In the contemporary environment it often happens that critical resources or information can be obtained only from one of these external sources. An officer may need to ne-

---

[13] The particular type of graduate school may not matter as much as the rigor of its curriculum. Whatever field is studied, the most important thing is that it inculcate a critical cast of mind, orientation to empirical observation, and an objective approach to testing hypotheses and selecting among competing alternatives. However, it *is* important that officers from the operations career field get this kind of education, along with officers from the specialty career fields.

[14] For evidence on the potential retention effects, see Wardynski et al. (2004).

gotiate with them to obtain something or influence them to take action. To argue persuasively in such a context, one needs to understand the structure of other institutions, the ways in which they operate, the way they see things, and the values they hold dear.

These same arguments apply, perhaps with even more force, when an Army leader must deal with foreign civilian populations and their leaders. For example, it has long been understood that special forces units are most effective when they understand the local culture and institutions; recent experiences in Afghanistan and Iraq reinforce this point. But more and more often this applies to conventional forces as well. Commanders in Bosnia found themselves immersed in local institutions and performing services akin to a local government. Units in Iraq need to gain intelligence from local sources. In those circumstances, U.S. leaders need to recognize the population's perceptions, belief systems, sacred and taboo symbols, rules by which they live, and the historical context as they see it. Without this cultural awareness, one may not be able to recognize novel features of the environment that matter to the mission.

Similar observations have been hammered home by others citing the experience in Iraq. An insightful exposition is provided by Scales (2004) in a recent discussion of the need for "culture-centric warfare." Scales points out that winning a war calls for much more than firepower and maneuver; it calls for building alliances, gaining the trust of civilian populations and elites, and influencing their opinions and perceptions. With those things accomplished, it is feasible to obtain intelligence, understand the enemy's intentions, and use that information effectively; without them, reliable information is scarce, it is hard to distinguish friend from foe, and operations proceed largely in the dark. In part, this is similar to "thinking like the enemy"—except that it might be better characterized as "thinking in a foreign context" because the leader needs to understand not only the enemy but also the neutral and friendly elements of the population.

For Americans, learning to think in a foreign context is difficult; foreign cultural features are generally unfamiliar and often counterintuitive.[15] As Scales mentions, the British grappled with the same problem during their long colonial period, and one of their solutions was to post promising officers abroad as "seconds," where they could absorb the local culture and interact with local leaders. That depth of experience paid off later—some say it still pays off for Britain in the current Iraq operation—but it cannot be done at the last minute. It must be planned for, recognized as valuable, and resourced and rewarded by the personnel and promotion systems.

[15] Probably the most famous observer of American culture to make this point was Alexis de Tocqueville in 1840 (republished in de Tocqueville, 2003). Recent expositions can be found in Lipset (1979, 1997).

Making Enough Time for Broadening Experiences

Unfortunately, in today's Army, few officers have much time to expand their breadth. A great deal of their time is taken up in operational assignments, with only modest time left for schooling. When overseas deployments add to the operational pace, time for study and cultural broadening is likely to be one of the first things forgone. Thus, long-term development is sacrificed in the interest of short-term requirements. This sacrifice is also encouraged by a military culture that prefers operational experience. Moreover, American culture has long been characterized by a kind of insularity regarding foreign languages and customs.[16] All of these factors operate to limit officers' exposure to things that would broaden their perspective.

What steps can be taken, then, to provide more time and broader exposure for future leaders? Drawing in part on Scales (2004), we suggest the following initiatives.

Professional military education. Army schools and courses need to focus more of their curriculum on other cultures, how they affect operational choices, and how to manage the peace within them. It would also be helpful if the student body included more representatives from other U.S. agencies and foreign nations, because much learning occurs in nonclassroom environments where students of varying backgrounds can interact informally. In this regard, one senior officer we interviewed observed that his best military education experience was his attendance at the Canadian forces' war college, where he was in a seminar with a bishop, government civilians, members of opposition political parties, and of course Canadian military officers. Discussing strategy with a group like this, he said, cannot help but broaden your perspective and sharpen your thinking.

Civilian graduate school. We argued earlier that civilian graduate education offers one of the best ways to pick up general reasoning skills. The same applies, perhaps more so, to absorbing knowledge of other cultures. Particularly for more senior leaders, the breadth conveyed by non-Army education is invaluable. Yet, the Army invests little in graduate education and even less in education for officers in the operations career field, even though they are most likely to be involved in overseas deployments where breadth is important.

Dedicated positions. At least some positions should be set aside for inculcating and deepening knowledge of other institutions and cultures. Scales, for instance, suggests building a "cadre of global scouts" who would learn a foreign culture and become comfortable with it. Similarly, he calls for a cadre of specially trained analysts who can interpret and disseminate the new information that such scouts would produce. Such specialists would be afforded more extensive education and interaction with officials of other agencies, other nations, and NGOs. The foundations for such a cadre could be found in the Army's Strategic Intelligence and Foreign Area Officer

[16] See again de Tocqueville and Lipset.

functional areas. Since these officers would be specialists, the Army would also need to educate its operational leaders to appreciate and capitalize on the capabilities of these cadres.[17]

Broadened training. Many of the other initiatives that we recommended in earlier sections can also be used to enhance cultural awareness across the entire force. For example, exercises can be modified to incorporate situations and uncertainties that are posed by operations in unfamiliar cultures. Distributed learning technology can help infuse lessons learned by the specialists and "global scouts" back into Army schools and CTCs. To make this work, the Army needs mechanisms to set aside individual "learning time" and to ensure that officers actually have duty time available for learning experiences.

More officers. It will be difficult to find the time, and the people to spend time, to master the new skills and knowledge that are clearly needed. It seems inescapable that the Army needs more officers if it is to man the force structure while still reserving enough people to undertake the tasks listed above. Adding officers would make it more feasible, for example, to send some on a mission as "seconds," to place more into positions selected for the wider perspective they afford, and to give more officers the opportunity for civilian education.

We are aware of statutory limitations on officer grade profiles, but we argue that their long-term relevance is now in question. The traditional grade pyramid does not provide enough people at the higher end when the leaders must first learn about a wholly new environment and then adapt their organizations to it. The additional officers should not be justified in terms of units they would lead, but rather in terms of functions they must perform to modernize the Army and the base of knowledge upon which it rests. Just as resources are needed to develop new technology and weapon systems, so are resources needed to develop the Army's people. We do not attempt to quantify the additional number of officers that may be needed, but we recommend that the Army review officer personnel structure, as well as officer career management systems, and seek changes—possibly in the longer term extending to legislative and budget changes—as needed.

Longer careers. Another major adaptation that might yield more time is to extend the length of military careers. Keeping an officer for, say, 25 to 30 years rather than 20 years makes sense particularly for specialists whose development takes many years and whose value is not sharply diminished by physical limitations that may come with age.[18] A policy long advocated by manpower analysts, this suggestion is

---

[17] It will prove impossible to imbue all officers with the same degrees of depth *and* breadth. As supporting skills become more sophisticated, the operational leader will increasingly have to develop a general appreciation for their importance but rely for details on a cadre of specialists with in-depth knowledge.

[18] Rising life expectancies and improved health care also suggest that soldiers, like many others, are staying fit longer in life.

now gaining interest in the Department of Defense and the Army.[19] Of course, guarantees and incentives would be needed to retain people, so such a change might well require further resources and legislation.

---

[19] See, for example, Fastabend and Simpson (2004), where it is argued that "an Army career today is simply too short to include all the necessary assignments and enough experience—particularly in the institutional Army—so that senior officers are confident of the intricacies of the institutional mechanism enough to attempt innovation." Longer careers have also been advocated at the Secretary of Defense level (Rhem, 2003).

CHAPTER SIX

Conclusions and Recommendations

Recent changes in the operational environment, national security strategy, and the Army's transformation have created profound effects on requirements for Army leaders. These effects have gradually become more visible over the past decade—since the interventions in Somalia and the Balkans—and ongoing operations in Iraq and Afghanistan suggest that they will continue to evolve for the foreseeable future. The broader international context, in which a central role is played by terrorism rather than hostile nation-states, confirms that the Army is now in a new world, one that places a premium on different skills and backgrounds than officers have striven to obtain in the past. Even when the Army operates in more "conventional" settings, the array of skills its leaders will need is broader than in the past.

Although the foundations of military leadership—character and values—are enduring traits whose importance has not changed, the nature of many other leadership attributes is evolving. In the field, the different facets of situations that now confront military leaders call for different operational skills. And, perhaps more fundamentally, these developments call for transformation in the range of intellectual abilities and the breadth of perspective that military leaders bring to their missions. In this chapter we review the implications of these changes in leadership requirements and summarize recommendations for adaptations in Army leader development.

Implications

We examined challenges posed by the new operational environment and analyzed the skills and background that might better enable leaders to meet those challenges. Our analysis pointed to three key areas of skills, knowledge, and ability.

Specific Operational Skills

Analysis of recent and ongoing operations suggested several skill areas that now require more emphasis. The situations that call for these skills vary significantly from what leaders confronted in the past. For example, today's environment makes it more important for a leader to quickly recognize an unconventional threat requiring force protection. The leader needs to be facile in urban operations and in applying a wider range of assets, including combined arms and joint capabilities. He needs to interact with civilian communities whose behavior is based on belief systems that are very different from Western norms and whose members may harbor suspicions of U.S. intent.

An appreciation of this complexity can be gleaned from reviewing the set of skill challenges that we identified in Chapter Three. This set includes some "traditional" military operational and technical skills, but it also calls for a more complete understanding and appreciation of socio-cultural factors that may influence the conduct or outcome of an operation. We identified nine areas in which the new environment poses challenges for leaders in the field:

- Joint and combined arms capabilities and operations
- Force protection
- Civilian presence on the battlefield
- Enemy capabilities
- Urban terrain
- Restrictive terrain
- Application of information technology
- Coalition partners
- Media presence

The requirement for these skills is more compelling because it arises from multiple causes. In Chapter Two, we cited three ways in which changes in the environment could give rise to greater skill requirements. First, the skill can simply increase in importance as it becomes more critical to the mission. Second, the situation may pose a more complex problem, requiring a greater degree of skill or nuance in reaching a "good enough decision, soon enough." Third, such skills are being demanded at lower echelons than in the past, confronting company commanders and even platoon leaders with problems that in the past would have been handled at more senior levels.

Developing all of these skills will be a challenge. Each skill area can be disaggregated into several more specific contributing or enabling subtasks, and in a training setting they are typically elaborated by variations in the circumstances under which they must be exercised. It will be difficult to develop all of them at one time, particularly in already-constrained unit environments.

To see how difficult that might be, we employed a model to explore officer career paths that would provide operational experience while still satisfying other demands (e.g., time attending professional schools or performing institutional functions). Overall, the results of the analysis were encouraging: the model yielded feasible solutions for every set of officer requirements we specified. The Army has latitude, therefore, to provide its leaders more time in field units and more exposure to operational positions, if it needs to do so. Within the constraints of the current position structure, it is possible to ensure that many officers get repeated operational assignments. We also found that the Army could build significant repetitive experience in *new* (or transforming) units, even to the point of developing a cadre of officers who get multiple leadership assignments in such units.

However, creating this degree of depth in operational experience comes at the expense of breadth. While the paths we modeled would produce a group of officers with high operational expertise, those same officers would lack much exposure to the Army's TDA institutions. Moreover, another group of officers would move along different paths, which would provide them little exposure to operational assignments beyond early years of service. Similar findings also apply to the distinction regarding service in transforming units: while the system can produce some officers with solid depth in new or transforming units, such a policy would simultaneously create another group of officers with little or no experience in such units.

This result prompted us to reconsider the strategy of relying primarily on unit experience to build operational skills. Instead, we have argued that the Army needs to leverage the capabilities of its institutions that support professional education and training. As we will elaborate below under "recommendations," this would involve reviewing and extending its entire set of learning tools: school curricula, distributed learning, Combat Training Center and home-station training regimens, and systems to collect performance data.

Intellectual and Cognitive Abilities

Recent years have seen renewed recognition within the Army that the modern environment calls not just for specific skills, but also for better-developed intellectual abilities. The changes outlined earlier in this report are transforming battle command (or, more generally, operational command—covering both battle and nonbattle situations) into a more complex and faster-paced problem. Under these circumstances, leaders need to use more rapid decision-making processes, to assess a novel situation and devise a course of action fitted to it. They need more facility in assimilating information, building a mental picture of the situation, adapting their previous plans, and quickly making and communicating a decision. Evolving U.S. military doctrine intensifies this need, because it envisions a stepped-up pace of operations across a complex and internetted battlefield, producing a welter of information and communications to be tracked and acted upon.

Faced with unfamiliar situations amid ambiguity and uncertainty, leaders have to short-cut the traditional but time-consuming decision-making processes taught in school. Instead, as explained in Chapter Two, they rely on rapid, "recognitional" decision-making processes. Research on actual decision processes has found that recognitional decision making is used successfully in many high-stress environments, but it requires several other competencies that support it:

- **Pattern recognition.** Reviewing past events and situations, seeking one that serves as a "model" for the current problem.
- **Understanding the situation.** Recognizing the key facets of the situation and the relevant conditions that affect outcomes—in Army terminology, achieving "situational understanding."
- **Simulation.** Considering one or more courses of action and assessing their likely outcomes.
- **Critical thinking.** Evaluating the likelihood that a particular action will produce a desired outcome—with sufficient objectivity to accept the possibility that the preferred course may fail.
- **Adaptability.** Being willing and able to adapt to an unfamiliar environment "on the fly" as a situation unfolds.
- **Breadth of experience.** Possessing a sufficient range of experience and knowledge to make the above processes work—having access to a wide range of empirical facts, knowledge of key conditions, and experience in predicting decision outcomes.

Today's environment calls for these skills, we have argued, in a way that the previous environment did not. During the Cold War, the nature of the threat and the surrounding circumstances were well known and intensively studied. Established war plans, battle positions, and operational doctrine helped to reduce the uncertainty inherent in any battlefield situation. In contrast, today's Army has been thrust into more unfamiliar situations and locales, without time to engage in thorough analysis of options or extended consideration of alternative courses of action, as called for in traditional doctrine for military decision making. Its leaders must make decisions in more varied situations—not only combat, but also stabilization, humanitarian, and peacekeeping missions—that inherently involve a broader range of factors.

Finally, leaders also need to engage in continuous learning and to become confident that they can acquire new skills and knowledge quickly when they confront new challenges. For example, the findings of the Army Training and Leader Development Panel (U.S. Army Training and Doctrine Command, 2001) point in this direction, as do vignettes and scenarios developed for intermediate-level education (Command and General Staff College, 2003).

How can these capabilities be developed? We have suggested that the above skills are inherently *cognitive* processes (modes of thinking). Thus, they are amenable to development in an academic, institutional setting, which permits reflection, study of complex constructs, and assessment of consequences in hypothetical situations.

Combining this intellectual grounding with the application of such skills, using simulations or practical exercises, will help to hone both the general and the specific skills. While some of this may be accomplished in fast-paced operational environments, units' practical constraints and time limits mean that the predominant role in developing intellectual skills must be played by academic institutions. As argued in Chapter Five, there is an important role in this process both for the Army's institutional schools and for graduate civilian education.

Breadth of Knowledge and Perspective

Breadth of perspective is becoming more important for leaders, for two main reasons that were discussed at length in Chapter Five. First, as important as the above cognitive skills are, their successful application rests on a base of wide experience and knowledge. Familiarity with a range of possible operational situations will give an officer a wider array of knowledge on which to draw in evaluating possible courses of action. The broader the base, the greater the likelihood a leader will find a similar situation on which to base such evaluations.

Second, familiarity with external institutions and cultures (e.g., other services, Joint commands, and government agencies) aids not only in planning and conducting operations, but also in gaining support from or influencing the actions of these external players. The same need for breadth applies to familiarity with foreign institutions, both military and civilian. Recent operational experiences of the U.S. military—in the Balkans, Afghanistan, and Iraq—have brought this point home. For example, units in the Balkans had to coordinate closely with local institutions and even provide services of a local government. Commanders in Iraq have found it essential to build local alliances, gain the trust of civilians, and influence the climate of opinion. Only through such activities can commanders gain necessary intelligence, appreciate enemy plans and modes of operation, and tell friends from enemies. In effect, the leader needs to understand not only the enemy but also the neutral and friendly elements of the population.

This kind of breadth is achievable only through contact with external institutions, and its importance reinforces the argument for greater exposure of officers to graduate education and broadening assignments outside the Army. In addition, as Scales (2004) has argued, leaders may need extensive in-country experience (such as a previous posting as a "second") and a network of Army cultural specialists who can provide specific information and perspective that no single officer could acquire by himself.

Recommendations

Having concentrated on changes in leader skills needed to keep pace with the evolving operating environment, we begin our recommendations by re-emphasizing the "something old": the Army should continue to acquire and develop leaders with the character traits and values that have always been the underpinning of effective leadership. Leaders who are not so grounded risk failure, regardless of technical or operational skills, because their subordinates will not follow them.

Beyond that essential base of leadership, our findings imply that considerably more needs to be done to develop leaders who are well prepared to meet the challenges of the contemporary environment and to continually learn and adapt to new circumstances. To accomplish that preparation, we suggest the following avenues of approach:

- Develop more **education modules** specifically designed to develop recognitional decision-making skills. These should pose both military and nonmilitary challenges.
- Develop more **practical exercise tools** that proffer a wider array of challenges, consistent with the contemporary operating environment, for use both in education modules (as above) and in field environments. The Army is already working to include more diverse challenges in its training modules at the Combat Training Centers.
- Capitalize on **distributed learning capabilities** to support predeployment (or, for that matter, postdeployment) familiarization as well as self-study programs. These tools can quickly take users through a variety of situations and thus can supplement other efforts to enhance breadth.
- Give officers **dedicated learning time**, in both academic settings (where it is easier) and in unit settings, to develop and broaden their skills.
- Provide greater opportunities for officers, especially those in the operations career field, to receive **advanced civil schooling.**[1] Graduate education inculcates depth in the key intellectual skills we have cited, and will also broaden perspectives in ways other experiences cannot.
- Broaden **professional military education**. Focus more on other institutions and cultures and how to cooperate with them. Increase opportunities to study in the schools of other services and nations, possibly as a supplement to the Army's professional academic curricula. Broaden exposure by including more foreign students, civilians, and officers from other services in Army schools.

[1] As we mentioned at the beginning of this report, these opportunities should be in addition to, and not at the expense of, current opportunities for officers in specialties found in the Army's officer functional areas.

- Set aside some **dedicated positions** specifically for the purpose of broadening officers who would not normally be designated for such positions. Officers could be "seconded" to these positions; while their primary purpose would be to learn, they could also make a direct contribution. An example would be a combat arms officer "seconded" to a position in strategic planning; a strategic planner could also be "seconded" as a deputy operations officer in a Joint command.
- **Lengthen careers.** Most of the alternatives above become more feasible if officers have more time to spend in each assignment and at each level. The current array of key developmental "gates" is so extensive as to be almost exclusively prescriptive. Adding additional developmental requirements (like "seconding" or more schooling) without adding more time would further complicate this situation.
- Access and develop a **larger inventory of officers.** This could go hand in hand with longer careers. Like longer careers, this would require major changes and resource investments, and thus would require a long-term planning horizon. However, it seems likely that many of the initiatives suggested above could be taken only with a larger base of officers to work with. We argue that while the current grade pyramid may have been suitable when it was designed, it may not allow enough officers to meet the requirements of the modern environment. At a minimum, the overall specifications for inventory and structure should be reviewed to assess whether they can meet modern requirements for breadth and depth.

Summing Up: The Need to Blend Broad Practical Experience With Intellectual Development

The challenges implied above are certainly not insurmountable. Probably the easiest thing to do is to develop the specific operational skills that we identified. Easier still will be developing the largely tactical subtasks that comprise these skill areas; they resemble skills that the Army has already been developing in its leaders. For example, the sample of subtasks that we listed for the force protection area closely parallels tasks already trained. In some cases, the same development merely needs to be provided at lower echelons and earlier in a career; in others there may be a need for greater sophistication or better training or education on specific new skills or technologies. In both types of cases the Army has a base of past experience from which to draw. The Army excels at compiling and systematizing lists of skills, enabling tasks, and subtasks like those we have illustrated. But implementing the ideas contained here—or others that grow out of them—will take time and money.

It will be harder to make changes that enhance intellectual skills and broaden officers' perspectives. Nevertheless, recent developments place a new premium on intellectual functions such as critical thinking and assembling information to make effective decisions in an alien and ambiguous environment. Those same developments point to an urgent need to give officers a broader understanding of cultures other than their own. We argue that learning about these new areas takes intellectual discipline, standardized instruction from academic experts, and, above all, time. Once again, this will take money because it will require more investments in schooling, more time for development during a career, and perhaps more officers in the force.

The aptitudes we have discussed in this work are challenging things to learn to an appropriate degree of sophistication—just as challenging as some of the complex skills in other professions such as medicine and law. Moreover, because military professionals are engaged in protecting vital national interests, the stakes are higher—although they are perhaps not as visible to outsiders, because American society is more familiar with professions it interacts with every day. So, as with other professions, continued investment is needed to impart both old and new skills to future generations. And, in line with the responsibility of professions to maintain the body of expert knowledge in their jurisdiction, the Army needs continued investment in its educational and professional systems to capture new concepts and skills, codify them, and maintain them for the future.

APPENDIX

Modeling Assignments and Experience

This appendix provides backup information about the model of assignments and experience described in Chapter Four. It describes the personnel structure assumed for Armor officers, the scoring schedules used to guide assignments to positions, and the optimization technique employed to generate solutions.

Personnel Structure and Flows

Requirements for Armor Officers

As outlined in Chapter Four, the model was built to recognize four types of positions that need to be filled by Armor officers at each grade from O-2 through O-4. To estimate the number of such positions, we began with official authorization data from the Army's Personnel Manning Authorization Document (PMAD) for the force as of September 2002. The PMAD shows numbers of authorized positions for each unit by the grade and occupational specialty required. We extracted records of positions calling for an Armor officer and distributed them into TOE versus TDA organizations according to the unit characteristics, as shown in Table A.1.

The table, however, is not complete in two respects. First, it does not split out the position types that we sought to identify (i.e., TOE leader versus TOE staff and enhanced TDA versus institutional TDA) because the PMAD does not make distinctions about specific positions.

Table A.1
Positions Requiring an Armor Officer, by Unit Type and Grade

Unit Type	O-2	O-3	O-4
TOE	826	456	113
TDA	46	266	151
Total	872	722	264

Second, the table does not account for other officer positions that are not specific to a branch. Such positions include "generalist" positions and functional area positions at the grade of captain. We aimed to allocate a proportionate fraction of such positions to the Armor branch, reasoning that each branch needs to contribute some officers (its "fair share") to meet such requirements. Below we describe how these requirements were quantified and incorporated into the position structure that we modeled.

Identifying TOE Leader Positions

We reviewed the entire set of armor units in the force structure and identified the leadership structure (from O-2 through O-4) for the primary types of units (such as divisional armor brigades and battalions, cavalry squadrons and troops, and armored cavalry regiments). Table A.2 summarizes types of units and the number of O-2, O-3, and O-4 leaders inferred from them.

Identifying TDA Enhanced Positions

We also needed to segregate enhanced positions within the TDA—that is, positions that contribute substantially to tactical skill development. To identify such jobs, we examined each unit in the TDA that had armor authorizations. Based on the unit's structure, function, and location we judged whether it was likely to provide significant opportunities to deepen or broaden one's tactical skills. For example, all of the positions for observer-controllers at the CTCs were designated as enhanced.

Table A.2
Number of TOE Leader Positions

		Number of Positions		
Type of Unit	Number of Units	O-2	O-3	O-4
Armor battalions	26	400	106	52
Heavy division cavalry squadrons	6	102	24	6
Light division cavalry squadrons	3	14	5	2
Separate cavalry troops	15	45	15	
Brigade HHCs	11	0	11	11
Cavalry regiment HHTs	3	0	3	6
Regimental cavalry squadrons	6	126	30	12
RSTA squadrons	2	28	10	4
Other unit types		45	22	1
Total Armor TOE unit leaders		760	226	94

HHC = Headquarters and Headquarters Company; HHT = Headquarters and Headquarters Troop; RSTA = Reconnaissance, Surveillance, and Target Acquisition.

We also applied that designation to some tactical instructors at Army schools and some officers providing tactical training to the Reserve Components. Clearly, not all positions in Army schools or RC support provide tactical experience. For example, leading a training company of new recruits or performing administrative duties in an RC unit would not warrant that designation. On the other hand, some jobs—such as teaching tactics in school or conducting field evaluations of unit training—do provide a considerable amount of experience. In such cases our expert consultants estimated the fraction of the unit's jobs—typically one-half—that would qualify.

We found no enhanced positions at the grade of O-2; lieutenants are simply too junior to fill such jobs or to profit from their benefits. However, we did find 117 O-3 positions that in our judgment should be considered enhanced: 38 observer-controller positions at the CTCs, 37 positions in tactical jobs at Army schools, and 42 positions providing training support to the RC. We also found 53 enhanced positions for O-4s: 29 positions at CTCs, 10 at schools, and 14 in RC training support.

Position Types for Armor Officer Requirements

We used the foregoing figures to determine the distribution of position types that specifically require an Armor officer. To obtain the TOE staff positions, we subtracted the number of TOE leaders from the TOE total, and to obtain the number of TDA institutional positions, we subtracted the number of TDA enhanced from the TDA total. Table A.3 shows the result.

Table A.3
Positions Requiring an Armor Officer, by Position Type and Grade

Position Type	O-2	O-3	O-4
TOE leader	760	226	94
TOE staff	66	230	19
TDA enhanced	0	117	53
TDA institutional	46	149	98
Total	872	722	264

Armor's Fair Share of Non-Branch-Specific Requirements

In addition to the figures in Table A.3, we needed to make allowance for Armor officers who would have to fill positions in the authorization documents that are not identified by branch. These positions include three major types:

- **Officer generalist.** These positions (also called branch immaterial) may be filled by any officer (but they must be filled).

- **Combat arms generalist.** These positions (also called combat arms immaterial) may be filled by any officer with a combat arms specialty.
- **Functional area** (at grade O-3). These positions call for a person with an initial specialization in a particular functional area (such as public information or acquisition). At the grade of O-3 officers may have declared such a functional area specialty but are still carried under their primary branch. Thus, some Armor officers (and officers from all other branches) will be needed to fill those jobs.

For each of these special groups of positions, we allocated the total number at that grade across all the branches and calculated the number of Armor officers needed so that the Armor branch could contribute its "fair share." Those fair-share figures are shown in Table A.4.[1] Adding Armor's fair share of the nonspecific requirements to the specific Armor requirements yields the distribution in Table A.5, which also appears in Chapter Four as Table 4.3.

Table A.4
Branch- and Non-Branch-Specific Requirements to Be Filled by Armor Officers

Authorization Type	O-2	O-3	O-4
Armor-specific requirements: Positions requiring an Armor officer	872	722	264
Non-branch-specific requirements: Armor's fair share			
Officer generalist	18	46	22
Combat arms generalist	11	78	46
Functional area	2	83	0
Total positions to be filled by Armor officers	903	929	332

Table A.5
Total Positions to Be Filled by Armor Officers, by Position Type and Grade

Position Type	O-2	O-3	O-4
TOE leader	760	226	94
TOE staff	77	279	29
Enhanced TDA	0	117	53
Institutional TDA	66	307	156
Total	903	929	332

NOTE: The total includes both Armor branch officers and Armor's "fair share" of generalist positions.

[1] Each of the fair-shared positions was attributed to either TOE staff (if the position was in a TOE unit) or TDA institutional (if the position was in a TDA unit) because we judged that TOE leadership and enhanced positions would generally be reserved for officers of a particular branch.

Positions in New Versus Old Units

One further specification by the model was the distinction between positions in "new" and "old" TOE units. The size of these groups is essentially arbitrary, since we used it as a parameter to govern different cases. As a starting point, we stipulated an initial complement of positions based on September 2002 authorizations for Armor officers in the two existing Stryker brigades and the two ACRs. These appeared to be likely candidates to deploy on new missions and possibly to undergo various structural changes that would pose new challenges. Table A.6 shows the division of Armor authorizations between these two classes of units, splitting out the TOE groups from Table A.5 above.

Table A.6
TOE Positions in New Versus Old Units

TOE Position	O-2			O-3			O-4		
	Old	New	Total	Old	New	Total	Old	New	Total
Leader	656	104	760	198	28	226	82	12	94
Staff	76	1	77	253	26	279	29	0	29
Total TOE	732	105	837	451	54	505	111	12	123

Generating Possible Paths

The number of paths builds up from the set of paths possible through each grade, which are governed by our assumptions concerning the acceptable sequences of jobs within and between grades. For example, consider the possible paths for lieutenants (grade O-2), as shown in Table 4.5, Chapter Four. We assume that lieutenants hold two jobs: the first is platoon leader (labeled PL) and the second is either platoon leader (again), TOE staff (labeled TOE), or institutional TDA (labeled INST). If platoon-leader jobs are categorized as in either the "new" or "old" part of the Army, then there are only two possibilities for a first job. Because the possibilities for a second job are the same if it is also platoon leader, there are $2 \times 2 = 4$ ways to complete lieutenancy if both jobs are as a platoon leader. If the second job is not platoon leader but instead is TOE staff, there are still two possibilities for the second job, "new" and "old," so there are $2 \times 2 = 4$ ways to complete lieutenancy. However, if the second job is in the institutional TDA, there are only $2 \times 1 = 2$ ways through the grade, because there is no "new-old" distinction within TDA positions (either institutional or enhanced). Taken together, this yields $4 + 4 + 2 = 10$ possible paths through the grade of lieutenant.

Similar logic identifies larger numbers of paths through the grades of captain and major, as illustrated in Table 4.6. In each of those grades, the first job is assumed to be a noncommand job in the TOE or a job in the institutional TDA. The second job includes those same two possibilities plus the possibility of a command job (company commander at O-3 or XO/S3 at O-4). The third job includes those same three possibilities plus the possibility of an "enhanced" job, but such enhanced jobs are possible only if the second job at the grade was a command position. If we distinguish "new" from "old" positions among command and TOE staff jobs, we can trace 81 different sequences through three jobs at O-3 and a similar 81 through three jobs at O-4.[2]

Across all three grades, this delineates 10 × 81 × 81 = 65,610 possible paths through O-2, O-3, and O-4. However, because we assume that officers will not hold XO/S3 positions as majors unless their experience includes command experience as captains, we can exclude 14,580 paths that would violate that assumption.[3] That leaves 51,030 paths through the three grades.

Flow of Officers Among Grades

To model the sequence of assignments for an officer cohort, we need to know how long officers remain in their positions at each segment and how many progress from one stage to the next. Chapter Four outlines the model assumptions about segment lengths within grades. Those assumptions, combined with the personnel structure in Table A.5, determine the rates of flow across grades and the retention rates from each grade to the next.

Table A.7 illustrates the resulting patterns. For example, at grade O-2 there are 903 positions to be filled. We assume they are filled by new entrants to the Army (that is, lieutenants who have just completed the basic officer course and been posted to a unit). The assumed career schedule has them serving two segments (occupying two consecutive positions) for 18 months each, after which some continue at grade O-3 within the Armor branch while others leave the Armor branch (some will leave the Army, while others will transfer elsewhere within the Army). Rows 2 and 3 of the table illustrate the result. Each lieutenant serves three years in assignments at grade O-2. Therefore, to fill the 903 O-2 positions the Army would need 301 entrants per year into the Armor branch.

---

[2] To determine the 81 paths, see Table 4.6. For each job labeled TOE (TOE staff) or CDR (commander), there are two possibilities: either new or old. For each job labeled INST (institutional TDA) or ENH (TDA enhanced), there is only one possibility. Thus pattern 1 leads to 2 × 2 × 2 = 8 possibilities; pattern 2 leads to 2 × 2 × 1 = 4 possibilities, pattern 5 leads to 2 × 1 × 1 = 2 possibilities, and so forth. The total number of possible paths, across all patterns, is 81.

[3] The excluded paths are those that contain no command job at O-3 but do contain an XO/S3 job at O-4. Inspecting Table 4.6 and applying the above rules, one can find 27 paths at O-3 that do not contain company command, and 54 paths at O-4 that do contain an XO/S3 job. Therefore, the number of theoretical paths that violate the assumption is 10 × 27 × 54 = 14,580.

Table A.7
Flow of Officers Among Grades

Grade	O-2	O-3	O-4
Positions to fill	903	929	332
Years in grade	3	6	4.5
Annual cohort	301	155	74
Losses at end of grade*	146	81	—
Continuing to next grade	155	74	—
Percent continuing to next grade	51.5	47.7	—

*May include movements into other branches or functional areas, or losses to the Army.

At the next grade, there are 929 positions to be filled by O-3s, but each O-3 serves for 6 years (three assignments of 24 months each). Therefore, only about 155 captains are needed to fill the 929 positions (because each of six annual cohorts contains 155 persons each). This means that among the 301 members of the lieutenant cohort, only 155 will continue within Armor as captains, while 146 will transition to other places.

Similar calculations apply to all three grades. The result, as shown in the last row of the table, fixes the O-2 to O-3 continuation rate at 51.5 percent, and the O-3 to O-4 continuation rate at 47.7 percent. We believe that these continuation rates are broadly consistent with observed patterns in officer cohorts, if one considers the cumulative rate of attrition over several years and the fact that many officers transition out of a specific branch into another position.

In any event, this is not a matter where the analyst is free to choose retention rates. The rates are driven by two factors: the personnel structure, which is fixed by the Army, and the length of time that officers remain in grade, which we took from recent observations of officer cohorts. Together those two things imply the retention rates that are derived here.

Experience Scoring Schedule

Given the personnel structure and the number of officers that are available at each segment, the model needed to determine what specific paths—sequences of position assignments—would fill all positions in accordance with certain rules. We specified those rules in two ways, both designed to parallel the way the Army prefers to operate.

First, we stipulated certain rules about when an officer can fill particular positions. This is described in Chapter Four. For example, we specified that every O-2 would begin as a platoon leader; that O-3s would serve as a company commander only during the second or third segment of their time at O-3; that O-4s would serve as an XO or S3 only during the second or third segment of their time at O-4; and that an officer could serve in an enhanced position only after serving in the leadership position at the same grade.

Those rules excluded many possible sequences and established only certain paths that could be followed at each grade, as explained in Chapter Four. However, they still leave a very large number of possible paths; that number reached 51,030 when we considered the distinction between new and old positions, each of which creates a distinct path that incorporates it. Therefore we needed a second set of rules, which we call preferences, and which would favor certain paths over others, just as the Army favors certain backgrounds over others when selecting candidates for leadership positions.

The model incorporated such preferences in the following way. For each path, imagine that the incumbents carry an experience profile showing which important experiences the officer has accumulated up to each segment of his career. In effect, the model kept track of accrued experience by assigning a 1 or 0 for each of the elements of experience shown in Table A.8.

When considering a group of candidates (actually, paths representing candidates), the model assessed the configuration of experiences that the candidates already possessed at that stage. Some experiences would be preferred for candidates about to enter certain assignments. For example, in filling a position of XO/S3, the Army would prefer—all other things equal—candidates who had multiple leadership experiences at O-2, greater amounts of TOE time at O-2 and O-3, experience in an enhanced position at O-3, and so forth.

Table A.8
Elements of Experience Profile

Grade	Experience	Symbol
O-2	Second leadership assignment (platoon leader or company XO)	2L
	TOE assignment (other than platoon leader)	TOE
O-3	Company commander	CDR
	Second assignment as company commander	CDR2
	Enhanced assignment	ENH
	1 TOE assignment (other than commander)	1TOE
	Second TOE assignment	2TOE
O-4	XO/S3	XO/S3
	1 TOE assignment (other than XO/S3)	1TOE
	Second TOE assignment	2TOE
Any grade	Experience in a "new" position	NEW

These preferences were embodied in a scoring matrix, exhibited in Table A.9. In that table each row represents a particular position that needs to be filled (say, CDR in an old unit, row 4 under O-3). The columns represent the vector of past experiences that an officer could possess (e.g., he could have had experience in the columns marked 2L, TOE, CDR, 2CDR, and so forth). The entries in the table show points awarded for each experience. For example, when filling a position as company commander in an old unit, a candidate would be given points as follows: three points for a second platoon leader assignment as a lieutenant; 1 point for a TOE staff assignment as a lieutenant; 3 points for a previous assignment as company commander; and one point each for a first or second assignment to a TOE staff position as a captain.

The schedule of points was designed to encourage selection of paths that yield maximum degrees of relevant experience in officers entering key positions, such as company commander, XO/S3, and enhanced positions. As can be seen by inspecting the table, it also was designed to create strong preferences for deep tactical experience among officers taking command of new units, and for officers who had experience in a new unit at a previous assignment.

Table A.9
Scoring for Experience Valuations

		Value of Past Experience for Prior Positions Held										
		O-2		O-3						O-4		
Grade	Position to Be Filled	2L	TOE	CDR	2CDR	ENH	1TOE	2TOE	XO/S3	1TOE	2TOE	New
O-2	PL old											0
	PL new											1
	TOE old											0
	TOE new											1
	INST											0
O-3	TOE old	1	2	2			2	2				0
	TOE new	2	2	2			2	3				1
	INST	1	1	2			1	1				0
	CDR old	3	1	3			1	1				0
	CDR new	4	1	4			1	2				1
	ENH	3	1	3			1					0
O-4	TOE old	1	1	1	1	1	2	2	2	2	2	0
	TOE new	1	1	2	2	2	2	3	2	2	3	1
	INST	1	1	1	1	1	1	1	2	1	1	0
	XO old	1	1	3	3	1	1	1	3	1	1	0
	XO new	1	1	3	4	2	1	2	4	1	2	1
	ENH	1	1	3	3	2	1	1	3	1		0

Optimization Method

In this section we provide a more technical description of the optimization approach and framework that was used in the model. This method permitted the model to select and display a single "optimal" solution that maximized point scores across all paths. The resulting displays are the solutions shown in the tables in Chapter Four.

In actual experience, we found that there were typically some alternative optimal solutions and many that were near-optimal. All were generally quite similar to the optimal solution displayed. For example, a near-optimal solution might have exactly the same set of paths as an optimal one, except for two paths where two positions were interchanged between the two solutions at one stage.

Overview

In this analysis we endeavor to select a "best" combination of career paths for a branch using a straightforward linear optimization model. We feed into the model a number of career paths, each one representing a sequence of jobs, one job per career stage. Every modeled officer enters and proceeds along a path until he leaves either the branch or the Army. To reflect equity and for simplicity, the simplest form of the model assumes that retention rates and times spent on jobs are the same for every career path. Each path provides some level of preparation for each job along the way, so each stage of each path has a point score that reflects both the importance of that stage's job and the quality of the preceding preparation. Finally, we tell the model how many jobs of each type must be filled at each grade.

Then the model uses linear optimization to find a combination of paths that would fill all the jobs and yield the largest total score—i.e., that would channel officers so that, collectively, they would be as fully qualified as possible for the jobs they would fill throughout the grades. If desired, additional points can be associated with each path to reflect preferences for the qualifications its officers would present when they became eligible for promotion beyond the grades modeled—i.e., when they exit the last career stage in the model. We use a so-called steady-state model, where a series of identical entering cohorts proceed through the same sequences of jobs year after year.

As demonstrated in this report, we have simplified things so that we model, for the Armor branch,

- 3 grades (lieutenant, captain, major);
- 8 career stages (2 at lieutenant, 3 at captain, 3 at major);
- 12 types of jobs;
- 51,030 career paths.

Using a desktop or laptop personal computer, in less than a minute the Generalized Algebraic Modeling System (GAMS) compiles the code, reads the input data, optimizes, and records its solution.

Below is the model's mathematical formulation, with the index sets described as we use them for the Armor branch.

Index Sets

g = grade ∈ *{O-2, O-3, O-4}*.

s = stage ∈ *{s1, s2, s3, . . . , s8}*.

j = job type ∈ *{PL1, PL2, OL1, OL2, CDR1, CDR2, XO1, XO2, TOE1, TOE2, ENH, Other}*.

p = path ∈ *{p00001, p00002, p0003, . . . , p51030}*

Parameters

Q_{ps} = points reflecting the quality of preparation for (and importance of) the job at stage s of path p,

R_s = fraction of path entrants who stay into career stage s (retention),

L_s = length of time (in months) spent in job at career stage s,

Y_{pgj} = average years an entrant to path p spends in job type j at grade g,

P_p = average total points accumulated for each entrant to path p,

M_{jg} = number of jobs of type j at grade g,

where Y_{pgj} and P_p are calculated from the other parameters as follows:

$$Y_{pgj} = \begin{cases} \sum\limits_{s \text{ in grade } g} R_s L_s / 12, & \text{if path } p \text{ has job type } j \text{ at stage } s \\ 0, & \text{otherwise} \end{cases}$$

$$P_p = \sum_s R_s Q_{ps} ,$$

Decision variables (nonnegative):

N_p = annual number of entrants to path p,

Objective function (total score to be maximized):

$$Z = \sum_{p} P_p N_p ,$$

Constraints (fill all types of jobs at all grades):

$$\sum_{p} Y_{pgj} N_p = M_{jg} ,$$

for each combination of j and g.

The optimization chooses the decision variables N_p to maximize the value of the objective function Z.

References

Army Infantry Journal Incorporated, *Infantry in Battle*, 2nd ed., 1939 (subsequently republished by the Marine Corps Association Bookstore, 1982).

Bennis, Warren, and Robert Thomas, *Geeks and Geezers*, Cambridge, MA: Harvard Business School Press, 2002.

Bloom, Benjamin S. (ed.), *Taxonomy of Educational Objectives: The Classification of Educational Goals: Handbook I, Cognitive Domain.* New York; Toronto: Longmans, Green, 1956.

Burk, James, "Expertise, Jurisdiction, and the Legitimacy of the Military Profession," in Lloyd J. Matthews et al. (eds.), *The Future of the Military Profession*, McGraw-Hill, 2002.

Cannon-Bowers, Janis, and Eduardo Salas (eds.), *Making Decisions Under Stress: Implications for Individual and Team Training*, American Psychological Association, 2000.

Cohen, Eliot A., "Defending America in the Twenty-First Century," *Foreign Affairs*, November-December 2000.

Cohen, Marvin S., Jared T. Freeman, and Bryan Thompson, "Critical Thinking Skills in Tactical Decision Making: A Model and Training Strategy," in Janis Cannon-Bowers and Eduardo Salas (eds.), *Making Decisions Under Stress: Implications for Individual and Team Training*, 2000.

Command and General Staff College, "Understanding Intermediate Level Education," U.S. Army Training and Doctrine Command News Service, July 2003, available at http://www.tradoc.army.mil/pao/TNSarchives/July03/ILE.html.

Cordesman, Anthony H., *The Lessons of Afghanistan*, Washington, D.C.: Center for Strategic and International Studies, 2002.

Cubic Defense Applications Group, *US Army Leader Development Campaign Plan: Officer Education System Needs Analysis, Final Report*, Fort Leavenworth, Kansas, July 2003.

Davis, Lynn E., and Jeremy Shapiro (eds.), *The U.S. Army and the New National Security Strategy*, Santa Monica, CA: RAND Corporation, MR-1657-A, 2003.

Davis, Paul K., and Lou Finch, *Defense Planning for the Post–Cold War Era*, Santa Monica, CA: RAND Corporation, MR-322-JS, 1993.

Department of the Army, *Leader Development for America's Army,* Department of the Army Pamphlet 350-58, Washington, D.C., 1994.

Department of the Army, *Staff Organization and Operations,* Field Manual FM 101-5, Washington, D.C., 1997.

Department of the Army, *Commissioned Officer Development and Career Management,* Department of the Army Pamphlet 600-3, Washington, D.C., 1998.

Department of the Army, *Army Leadership,* Field Manual FM 22-100, Washington, D.C., 1999.

Department of the Army, Objective Force Task Force, *The Objective Force in 2015,* White Paper, 8 December 2002.

Department of the Army, *Training the Force,* Field Manual FM 7-0, Washington, D.C., 2002.

Department of the Army [Secretary and Chief of Staff, U.S. Army], *United States Army Transformation Roadmap,* Washington, D.C., November 2003.

Dobbins, James, Keith Crane, Seth G. Jones, John G. McGinn, Andrew Rathmell, Rollie Lal, Brett Steele, Rachel M. Swanger, Richard Teltschik, and Anga Timilsina, *The RAND History of Nation-Building,* Santa Monica, CA: RAND Corporation, MG-304/1-RC, 2005.

Doubler, Michael D., *Closing With the Enemy: How GIs Fought the War in Europe (1944–1945*), Kansas University Press, 1994.

Fastabend, David A., and Robert H. Simpson, "The Imperative for a Culture of Innovation in the U.S. Army: Adapt or Die," *Army Magazine,* February 2004.

Fielder, Fred, *Leadership Experience and Leadership Performance,* Alexandria, VA: Army Research Institute, 1994.

Fontenot, Gregory, E.J. Degen, and David Tohn, *On Point: The U.S. Army in Operation Iraqi Freedom,* Fort Leavenworth, KS: Combat Studies Institute Press, 2004.

Gilmore, Gerry J., "'Significant Portion' of Troop Shifts to Be Europe-Based Forces," *American Forces Information Service,* news article, August 16, 2004, available at http://www.defenselink.mil/news/Aug2004.

Glenn, Russell, *Marching Under Darkening Skies,* Santa Monica, CA: RAND Corporation, MR-1007, 1998.

Goldman, Charles A., Bruce R. Orvis, Michael G. Mattock, and Dorothy A. Smith, with Rodger Madison and Laurie McDonald, *Staffing Army ROTC at Colleges and Universities: Alternatives for Reducing the Use of Active-Duty Soldiers,* Santa Monica, CA: RAND Corporation, MR-992-A, 1999.

Hamburger, Kenneth E. (ed.), *Leadership in Combat: An Historical Appraisal,* West Point, NY: United States Military Academy, Department of History, 1984.

Jones, Seth G., Jeremy Wilson, Andrew Rathmell, and Kevin Jack Riley, *Establishing Law and Order After Conflict,* Santa Monica, CA: RAND Corporation, MG-374-RC, 2005.

Klein, Gary, *The Sources of Power: How People Make Decisions*, Massachusetts Institute of Technology, 1998.

Leed, Maren, *Keeping the Warfighting Edge: An Empirical Analysis of Army Officers' Tactical Expertise*, Santa Monica, CA: RAND Corporation, MR-1378-A, 2002.

Leonard, Henry A., John D. Winkler, Anders Hove, Emile Ettedgui, Michael G. Shanley, and Jerry M. Sollinger, *Enhancing Stability and Professional Development Using Distance Learning*, Santa Monica, CA: RAND Corporation, MR-1317-A, 2001.

Lipset, Seymour Martin, *The First New Nation: The United States in Historical and Comparative Perspective*, New York: W.W. Norton, 1979.

Lipset, Seymour Martin, *American Exceptionalism: A Double-Edged Sword*, New York: W.W. Norton, 1997.

Lowe, Christian, "Lieutenant Relishes Role as Neighborhood 'Mayor,'" *Army Times*, July 7, 2003.

Matthews, Lloyd J. (ed.), Don M. Snider, and Gayle L. Watkins, *The Future of the Military Profession*, McGraw-Hill, 2002.

Moses, Franklin L., *Training Challenges for Digitization,* U.S. Army Research Institute, Special Report 47, June 2001.

Naylor, Sean D., "For Now, Cops First, Soldiers Second," *Army Times*, May 26, 2003.

Office of the Secretary of Defense [Director, Force Transformation], *Military Transformation: A Strategic Approach*, Department of Defense, Washington, D.C., 2003.

OPMS [Officer Personnel Management System] XXI Task Force, *OPMS XXI Final Report*, unpublished report prepared for the Army Chief of Staff, Office of the Deputy Chief of Staff for Personnel, 1997.

Rhem, Kathleen T., "Up-or-Out Personnel Policy 'Lousy Idea,' Rumsfeld Tells Sailors," *American Forces Information Service*, news article, November 15, 2003, available at http://www.dod.gov/news/Nov2003.

Rommel, Erwin (ed. B.H. Liddell Hart), *The Rommel Papers,* Random House, 1987.

Scales, Robert, *Army Transformation: Implications for the Future,* statement before the U.S. House Armed Services Committee, July 15, 2004.

Setear J., C.H. Builder, M.D. Baccus, and W. Madewel, *The Army in a Changing World: The Role of Organizational Vision*, Santa Monica, CA: RAND Corporation, R-3882, 1990.

Simon, Herbert A., *Models of Thought*, New Haven: Yale University Press, 1979.

Simon, Herbert A., *Administrative Behavior: A Study of Decision-Making Processes in Administrative Organization*, 3rd ed., New York: The Free Press, 1976. Originally published 1945.

Snider, Don M., briefing presented to the Army's Officership Doctrinal Integration Conference, 3–5 February 2003.

Snider, Don M., and Gayle L. Watkins, "Introduction," in Lloyd J. Matthews et al., *The Future of the Army Profession*, 2002.

Schirmer, Peter, Dina G. Levy, Harry Thie, Joy S. Moini, Margaret C. Harrell, Kimberly Curry, Kevin Brancato, and Megan Abbott, *New Paths to Success: Determining Career Alternatives for Field-Grade Officers*, Santa Monica, CA: RAND Corporation, MG-117-OSD, 2004.

Sortor, Ronald E., and J. Michael Polich, *Deployments and Army Personnel Tempo*, Santa Monica, CA: RAND Corporation, MR-1417-A, 2001.

De Tocqueville, Alexis, *Democracy in America*, Penguin Books, 2003.

U.S. Joint Staff, Director for Strategic Plans and Policy, J-5, *Joint Vision 2020*, Washington, D.C.: U.S. Government Printing Office, 2000.

U.S. Army Training and Doctrine Command, *White Paper: Capturing the Operational Environment,* Fort Leavenworth, Kansas, February 2000.

U.S. Army Training and Doctrine Command, *The Army Training and Leader Development Panel, Officer Study, Report to the Army,* U.S. Army Combined Arms Center, Fort Leavenworth, Kansas, 2001, available at http://www.army.mil/features/ATLD/report.pdf

U.S. Army Training and Doctrine Command, *The United States Army Objective Force: Operational and Organizational Plan for Maneuver Unit of Action*, TRADOC Pamphlet 525-3-90/O&O, Fort Monroe, Virginia, 22 July 2002.

U.S. Army Training and Doctrine Command, *The Operational Environment and Threat,* Combat Training Center Seminar Briefing, Deputy Chief of Staff for Intelligence, TRADOC [Army Training and Doctrine Command], Fort Monroe, Virginia, 3 February 2003.

Vinson, Mark E., "Structuring the Army for Full-Spectrum Readiness," *Parameters*, Summer 2000, pp. 19–32.

Von Mellenthin, F.W., *Panzer Battles*, Ballantine Books, 1985.

Wass de Czege, Huba, *Why We Have Leaders,* presentation prepared for the 1986 Army-Wide Leadership Conference, Fort Leavenworth, Kansas, December 1986.

Wardynski, Casey, Marc Wehmeyer, David Lyle, and Luke Gallagher, *Building a Bench of High-Performance Leaders—Effective, Efficient, and Feasible Army Level Policy Options,* West Point, NY: United States Military Academy Office of Economic and Manpower Analysis, 2004.